**DECOLONIZATION
AND THE DECOLONIZED**

WORKS BY ALBERT MEMMI

À Contre-courants
Agar, un roman
The Colonizer and the Colonized
Dependence: A Sketch for a Portrait of the Dependent
Dominated Man: Notes toward a Portrait
The Pillar of Salt
Portrait of a Jew
Racism
The Scorpion; or, The Imaginary Confession

ALBERT MEMMI

Decolonization
and Decolonized
the

Translated by Robert Bononno

UNIVERSITY OF MINNESOTA PRESS
Minneapolis • London

The University of Minnesota Press gratefully acknowledges financial assistance for the translation of this book provided by the French Ministry of Culture–Centre national du livre. Ouvrage publié avec le concours du Ministère français chargé de la culture–Centre national du Livre.

First published in France as *Portrait du décolonisé: arabo-musulman et de quelques autres,* copyright 2004 Éditions Gallimard, Paris.

Copyright 2006 by Robert Bononno

All rights reserved. No part of this publication may be reproduced, stored in a retrieval system, or transmitted, in any form or by any means, electronic, mechanical, photocopying, recording, or otherwise, without the prior written permission of the publisher.

Published by the University of Minnesota Press
111 Third Avenue South, Suite 290
Minneapolis, MN 55401-2520
http://www.upress.umn.edu

Library of Congress Cataloging-in-Publication Data
Memmi, Albert.
   [Portrait du décolonisé arabo-musulman et de quelques autres. English]
   Decolonization and the decolonized / Albert Memmi ; translated by Robert
Bononno.
   p. cm.
   First published in France as *Portrait du décolonisé: arabo-musulman et de quelques autres,* copyright 2004 Éditions Gallimard, Paris.
   Includes bibliographical references.
   ISBN-13: 978-0-8166-4734-7 (hc : alk. paper)   ISBN-10: 0-8166-4734-8 (hc : alk. paper)
   ISBN-13: 978-0-8166-4735-4 (pb : alk. paper)   ISBN-10: 0-8166-4735-6 (pb : alk. paper)
   1. Postcolonialism—Arab countries. 2. Hybridity (Social sciences)—Arab countries.
3. Ethnopsychology—Arab countries. 4. National characteristics, Arab. 5. Arab countries—Emigration and immigration. 6. Arabs—Foreign countries. I. Bononno, Robert.
II. Title.
   JV51.M42b 2006
   325´.309174927—dc22
                             2006013903

Printed in the United States of America on acid-free paper
The University of Minnesota is an equal-opportunity educator and employer.

12   11   10   09   08   07   06   10   9   8   7   6   5   4   3   2   1

Contents

vii Acknowledgments

ix Introduction

1 The New Citizen

THE GREAT DISILLUSION • A PARADOXICAL POVERTY •
CORRUPTION • IMPOSTERS AND POTENTATES • TYRANTS,
ZEALOTS, AND SOLDIERS • DIVERSIONS, EXCUSES, AND
MYTHS • A CONVENIENT CONFLICT • THE FAILURE OF
THE INTELLECTUALS • FICTION AND REALITY • CULTURAL
LETHARGY • THE CLERICS' PLOT • FROM REPRESSION
TO VIOLENCE • A NATION BORN TOO LATE • NATIONS
WITHOUT LAW • A SICK SOCIETY • GOING ABROAD

71 The Immigrant

THE BLESSINGS OF EXILE • FAILURE TWICE OVER • A NEW
REFRAIN • THE GHETTO • HEAD SCARVES AND *MÉTISSAGE*
• HUMILIATION • FROM HUMILIATION TO RESENTMENT
• THE SOLIDARITY OF THE VANQUISHED • CORPORATE
IDENTITY • ABANDONING THE MYTH OF RETURN • THE
IMMIGRANT'S SON • THE ZOMBIE • FROM EXCLUSION
TO DELINQUENCY • QUESTIONING INTEGRATION •
RECIPROCAL DEPENDENCE • THE LANGUORS OF EUROPE
• HOPE FOR THE DECOLONIZED? • TOWARD A NEW WORLD

145 Afterword

Acknowledgments

I wish to thank Agnès Guy, Henri Lopes, Afifa Marzouki, Alicia Duvojné Ortiz, and Sabia Samaï for their attention to those parts of the book dealing with Black Africa, the Maghreb, Latin America, and the suburban slums.

I would especially like to thank Pierre Maillot, whose friendly suggestions have been particularly useful.

Introduction

Rarely have I had so little desire to write a book. For in writing *Decolonization and the Decolonized,* I feared that my arguments would go unheard or be distorted, or might compound the problems faced by still fragile societies in need of our support. Nevertheless, when all was said and done, I felt there was an urgent need that formerly colonized peoples have an opportunity to hear a voice other than that of their so-called allies. When, in the 1950s, I wrote *The Colonizer and the Colonized,* I knew that some of my readers would refuse to follow me. Liberals, for example, like the highly esteemed Pierre Mendès-France, who felt that once the necessary reforms had been established, the colonized would abandon their quest for independence; or Marxists, who claimed, as usual, that decolonization consisted primarily in economic demands. I believed they were wrong and that the situation was more complex than that. I also expected to hear from another segment of popular opinion, one that defended the endurance of colonization; but that segment, aside from its errors of judgment, I enjoyed contradicting. I consoled myself for so many potential misunderstandings by convincing myself that I would at least obtain the complete approval of the oppressed; which turned out to be the case. But in writing *Decolonization*

ix

INTRODUCTION

and the Decolonized, I fear I have managed to annoy just about everyone. How often was it suggested to me—with a tone of irony or skepticism—that I should rather try to depict what has become of the colonized. In other words, that my efforts were misplaced. And certainly, at times, I did ask myself that very question; but this was not the source of my hesitation. It seemed to me that perhaps what was needed was to allow time to do its work.

Several decades have now passed. It is finally possible to evaluate what has been lost and gained, and possibly to draw certain conclusions for the future.

From the outset it must be acknowledged that, far from underestimating the benefits of the liberty conquered, or reconquered, by colonized peoples, it is important to emphasize all that remains to be done. National and ethnic liberation movements were legitimate and urgently needed, similar to the women's movement of today. But while we must continue to work so that all nations, young and old, all minorities finally stand as equals among equals, it is no less necessary, for that very reason, to examine why those pitched battles did not always produce the anticipated results. I concluded *The Colonizer and the Colonized* with the words "Having reconquered all his dimensions, the former colonized will have become a man like any other," but I also added "with all the ups and downs of all men to be sure." Clearly, the downside continues to play a preponderant role.

During the first years of independence, attentive and well-meaning observers grew concerned about the persistent poverty of formerly colonized peoples. Fifty years later nothing really seems to have changed, except for the worse. Their analysis was focused primarily on Black Africa. It is now obvious that the majority of Arab-Muslim and Latin American states, including those with sufficient resources, are not doing

x

INTRODUCTION

much better. In spite of the sometimes spectacular growth of individual states, malnutrition, famine, and endless political crises also affect a number of Asian countries. Widespread corruption and tyranny and the resulting tendency to use force, the restriction of intellectual growth through the adherence to long-standing tradition, violence toward women, xenophobia, and the persecution of minorities — there seems to be no end to the pustulent sores weakening these young nations. Why such failures? What are the consequences on the physiognomy and behavior of the formerly colonized? These are the kinds of questions this portrait of contemporary decolonization attempts to answer.

Like *The Colonizer and the Colonized*, this work, which is to some extent its continuation, is neither a political tract nor a utopian dream. Except for the final pages, which examine future perspectives and are presented as a series of hypotheses, the book is an assessment of the present situation. It attempts to describe a new reality, the reality of people who were once but are no longer colonized, or nearly so, who sometimes continue to believe they are, and who are part of the unfolding drama of history.

As before, I have relied on the Arab-Muslim model, more specifically, the Maghreb. Simply because that is the region I know best, having been born and raised there, and having retained, in spite of the current difficulties, strong affiliations and friendships. And also because it presents some of the most intractable problems in the world. However, as often as possible I have made use of other experiences, and made comparisons with South America, Asia, and Black Africa in particular. I would be dishonest if I did not acknowledge that it is my hope that the majority of the decolonized recognize themselves in this portrait, at least partially.

Naturally, every situation is unique. The decolonization

xi

INTRODUCTION

of Latin America took place at the beginning of the nineteenth century. The current inhabitants are primarily of mixed race and often the descendants of the colonizers; they are Christians, which is why there are no religious problems, as in parts of Black Africa. Black Africans have experienced slavery as well as colonization; French-speaking Africa does not coincide with English-speaking Africa. However, generally speaking, I tend to think that the mechanisms governing decolonization, like those governing colonization, are, aside from local differences, relatively uniform. That is why I have retained the expression "third world," even if the general tendency is to replace it by "countries of the South," which is too restrictive, geographic in scope, and not really meaningful for my purpose—and because I have not found a better one.

For the most part, this portrait concentrates on three figures: the ex-colonized, who has remained in his country and become a new citizen of an independent state; the immigrant, who has chosen to live abroad, often in the former colonizing nation; and the sons and daughters of the immigrant, born in the country where their parents have settled. Although they do not coincide with one another, they are three aspects of the same character, and this three-part division forms the basis of my book.

I realize that I open myself up to criticism for my rather bleak presentation. I have, similarly, been criticized for what I have referred to as the *deprivation* of the colonized, the misfortune of being Jewish, or the fragile situation of the majority of women. Some preferred to believe that the proletariat was the paragon of virtue and woman, the human being par excellence. Like the colonized, the decolonized is not a saint; how could he be and continue to live through such an agitated period of his history?

In writing this book it was necessary to satirize certain

xii

INTRODUCTION

taboos. This examination should have been undertaken by the elites in the countries under discussion, but for reasons that also required explanation, they seem to have been overcome by a strange inability to think or act, so that, through their own acquiescence, they have given free rein to the most backward among them. Yet it is this critical combat that has given the democratic societies of the West their contemporary shape and triumphant dynamism.

The defenders of the formerly colonized are hardly much more helpful in this difficult and essential enterprise. Instead of promoting democrats, or joining them, in the wake of an understandable postcolonial guilt, they feel compelled to observe a kind of comprehensive complacency that tends toward demagoguery. This guilt becomes noxious when it leads to blindness, as it has with certain remorseful Christians and primitive Marxists. Catholics, wracked by doubt, feel it is morally necessary, and convenient, to encourage the formerly colonized in retrograde beliefs and practices. Voltaireans, who would willingly devour a priest alive, show deference toward imams. Associations established to defend secularism, after a long struggle against social and clerical conservatives, find that immigrants do not always make the distinction between the religious and the secular, and wonder whether or not the very foundations of the Republic need to be reconsidered. At the other extreme are those who consider that catastrophe was narrowly averted, that Europe will inevitably experience other "Kosovos." The embarrassment, if not the hypocrisy, of governments, their ineffectiveness in their dealings with new nations or in addressing the problems of immigrants, are of equal importance. There is work to be done in describing the interaction between former colonizers and the formerly colonized; although this was not my purpose, some aspects of such an analysis can be found here. More than a precautionary

INTRODUCTION

compassion is needed if we are to help decolonized peoples; we must also acknowledge and speak the truth to them, because we feel they are worthy of hearing it.

Finally, I remain convinced that the best way of correcting such failures is to make an accurate assessment of them, which is what I have tried to do. This seemed to me the best way of assisting those who were once colonized—and their inevitable partners as well.

The New Citizen

The Great Disillusion

The end of colonization should have brought with it freedom and prosperity. The colonized would give birth to the citizen, master of his political, economic, and cultural destiny. After decades of imposed ignorance, his country, now free, would affirm its sovereignty. Opulent or indigent, it would reap the rewards of its labor, of its soil and subsoil. Once its native genius was given free rein, the use of its recovered language would allow native culture to flourish.

Unfortunately, in most cases, the long anticipated period of freedom, won at the cost of terrible suffering, brought with it poverty and corruption, violence, and sometimes chaos. Those days are long gone, lost in the fog of memory, when, with the dawn of independence—something the younger generations have not experienced—the national leader, finally released from prison, entered the capital to the screams of women and the shouts of men, barely able to hold back their tears. The slogans of national unity, heard at a time when everyone felt as if they were members of the same family, have been extinguished, and the faces we see are the pale faces of egotism.

Naturally, it is reassuring for a people to be governed by leaders of its own; flattering to see its flag flapping in the wind in place of that of the colonizers, to be able to call upon a nascent armed forces, have its own currency, be represented

THE NEW CITIZEN

among the family of nations by ambassadors and diplomats from the homeland. But not everyone can be an ambassador or consul, not everyone is gifted enough to take advantage of the new climate. Certainly, we shouldn't underestimate efforts that bear fruit, but, for the majority, things haven't changed much. There has been a change of masters, but, like new leeches, the new ruling classes are often greedier than the old.

In truth, for the economy at least, this could have been anticipated. Whenever a leader of the anticolonial struggle was asked for details about his social program, he would respond vaguely, "The time is not right; we'll know better later, after the liberation." The time may not have been right, there were other urgent matters to attend to, but since then nothing much has happened. We might have expected, in the Arab countries at least, that the middle class, the only one capable because of its skills, its technical and cultural education, would have taken care of the administration of national business matters in the interests of its people. This was utopian. Instead, this class exacted privileges for itself and developed a political and administrative system to protect them. In the colonies it was said, sarcastically, that the job of the sheiks, local leaders recruited from the ranks of the colonized, was to grab the goats by the horns so they could be milked more easily, goats here symbolizing the colonized. The new sheiks, appointed by their government after independence, serve their leaders in that same capacity. Worse than the hypocrisy of ideology, relations between classes, like relations with peoples, are governed by rapine rather than philanthropy: Why should the local middle class be less disinterested than anywhere else? When have the privileged ever given up their privileges except under the threat of losing them?

THE NEW CITIZEN

A Paradoxical Poverty

Poverty, however, is not fatal, and a handful of examples demonstrate this. Tunisia, a small, non-oil-producing country (which may be a blessing in disguise), China, and India have made important progress in the struggle against poverty. What is still needed is the will to conquer it and the intelligence to develop the means. A few years ago, during a friendly meeting with the ambassador of a third-world nation, we happened to ask about his country's efforts to fight poverty. It seemed to us that this would be a priority. We were naive. He answered us, with some embarrassment, by listing the other efforts, equally important as far as he was concerned, that his government was responsible for. We had just discovered, much to our astonishment, that for a number of third-world governments, the elimination of poverty was not their major concern; they did not consider it the principal problem facing their people. Yet, from the evidence, poverty leads to and helps prolong ignorance and superstition, stagnant forms of social behavior, the absence of democracy, poor hygiene, sickness, and death.

Certainly there are degrees of poverty. The Maghrebian or Egyptian fellah can eat his daily vegetable couscous or bowl of beans; in some places people do not even have that much. In Black Africa the tourist who takes the trouble to stray from his air-conditioned hotel or the luxurious out-of-the-way camps used by vacationers, and dares to enter the local homes, will be horrified by what he finds. How could he forget those smoke-filled interiors where the women cook directly on the beaten earth, rinsing their food in basins of dirty water? Or the children, as attractive as ebony dolls, dirty and partially dressed, many of whom will soon become statistics, numbering among the premature dead. Or the

THE NEW CITIZEN

beautiful young women, as graceful as gazelles, who will die in childbirth for lack of antibiotics (antibiotics have not always existed but they exist now and could save them). Along the main roads one sees matronly women, wrapped in fat, seated throughout the day behind tables of cheap planks, waiting for buyers for their few pounds of fruit or vegetables, the proceeds from which they'll use to buy food for the family dinner and some fuel for the lamps and stove. If our tourist wanders into the country's interior, he will discover malnutrition and disease everywhere he goes, and, of course, an archaic culture, magical practices, and the imaginative fantasies that nourish the people but that in turn help to keep them poor.

What is the reason for such long-standing crises? It may be understandable for countries lacking natural resources or adequate social and governmental support, but why in Venezuela and Nigeria, which are loaded with oil, does at least 20 percent of the population live below the threshold of poverty? Fifty percent of the inhabitants of Zimbabwe, where diamonds are mined, live in the most dire poverty. In wealthy Argentina, which could feed four or five times its own population, children faint from hunger in the schools and streets. Professionals are reduced to raising chickens in their bathrooms, selling cakes baked by their wives. In North Korea a third of the population survives only through food support from around the world. In India, one of the leading global producers of grains, poverty has until recently been too great to measure. Not only do these countries not grow, they often become impoverished. Some wag has suggested referring to them as "countries on the road to underdevelopment." But the expression could easily be applied to Algeria, Kuwait, even Saudi Arabia, whose per capita income has decreased 60 percent since 1980. Why has Algeria, which discovered its immense hydrocarbon wealth at the same time as Norway,

THE NEW CITIZEN

remained in an alarming state of poverty, while Norway, once one of the poorest countries in Europe, is now one of the most developed? Why has Mexico, also an oil-producing country and one of the leading beneficiaries of tourist dollars, been subject to periodic crises that have led it to the brink of bankruptcy and forced it to beg for debt relief from foreign debtors? In 2003 Argentina declared that it would unilaterally cancel three-quarters of its debt; between individuals this would be considered fraud and subject to prosecution.

Such is the paradox. Generally speaking, the third world is poor and dying of starvation. Potentially it has the wherewithal to supply the needs of all its citizens, but lacks organization and suffers from an ineffective, absurd, and scandal-ridden system of distribution. Why in the Middle East, a world that is still based on a feudal order, do certain Bedouin families possess such fabulous wealth from lands where they arrived more or less by accident? We could, it is true, ask the same question about the American settlers. Why is it that all members of the human community do not share equally in the gifts provided by nature? But I'd like to put that utopia aside for now. The fact remains that any continent, no matter how poor it may appear, contains the wherewithal to feed all its inhabitants. So why the present disaster?

Corruption

We can discuss at length the reasons for this tragic absurdity. They include technological delays, lack of enough trained technicians, inadequate intellectual support structures, backward institutions and cultures, fierce international competition, and uncooperative weather patterns. But one remains common to nearly all of them: corruption. Corruption is not limited to the third world; it is, or has become, universal. It

7

THE NEW CITIZEN

has affected even the oldest and most respectable Western nations, where scandal follows scandal, facilitated by the speed and suddenness of exchange. The stock market, the pivot and mirror of the state of an economy, and which should regulate and manage various interests, has become a machine for punishing the weakest and least informed, therefore, indirectly the poorest. But corruption remains shameful and disguised. In young nations, less sensitive in this respect, it is cynical and brutal, a kind of generalized system of payoffs, accepted or tolerated by everyone, a kind of institution. The corruption ranges from the policeman, to whom the grocery store owner gives a bunch of leeks or artichokes so he will be left in peace, or the highway patrolman who collects a sort of personalized highway "toll," all the way up to the large importers of agricultural machinery, who pay dividends to bureaucrats to obtain import licenses or a friendly meeting with a minister. When the past president of Madagascar began draining the country on a regular basis, it was obvious to everyone, and came with the blessing of France, supposedly the country's great protector and friend. Corruption is universal and affects everything and everyone, including the young, who receive a handful of reassuring crumbs and are complicit, complacent, or resigned victims. It affects rich and poor countries alike, but the greatest corruption frequently accompanies the greatest poverty. Nigeria, one of the richest countries in Africa, has one of the poorest populations in the world and, at the same time, one of the highest levels of corruption. Cameroon, which may be the most corrupt country on the planet, has the greatest number of people living in poverty. More generally, if it were necessary to classify nations, the nations of Black Africa would come out on top for this destructive combination of poverty and corruption.

THE NEW CITIZEN

Corruption is not just morally blameworthy, it expresses and helps maintain the breakdown of the social fabric. It negates creativity and impedes innovation, which requires initiative and effort. Instead of establishing companies, it is easier and more immediately profitable to demand outlandish kickbacks on transactions, sometimes fictive, or on international aid, a large part of which never reaches its destination. It is easier to pretend, by cooking the books or offering bribes, to launch extensive capital works programs that will never be completed or even begun; easier to build garish hotels that remain half empty using government loans that will never be paid back, through financial schemes that would be legally actionable if government agencies didn't simply close their eyes to what was happening around them. This kind of manipulation goes on all over Africa, Muslim and Christian, in Catholic Mexico as well as the virtuous Islamic Republic of Iran and the lay democracy of India. Periodically, a head of state will solemnly announce his intention to fight rampant corruption—as if the thieves were promising to restore order. Arsène Lupin disguised as the chief of police.

By the same token, with all the scheming and the insidious laxity, the fortuitous and too easily acquired wealth is rarely reinvested in the country, which would be the norm in a healthy economy. It is estimated that between 40 and 80 percent of the proceeds are—surreptitiously but with the tacit agreement of foreign governments, which also benefit—transferred to secret accounts abroad. At present no one has estimated the amount of oil income that is similarly converted into real-estate investments in London and New York. The border between public and private finance is often difficult to determine. At the time of the Gulf War, it was shown (as was already known) that the head of state, Saddam

Hussein, was one of the world's richest men. It's unlikely that he made his fortune in his family's village.

The continuous, unproductive bloodletting prevents the creation of domestic industries, which is today essential for autonomous development. Moreover—and this is part of the same vicious circle—the lack of development means there is little or no opportunity for investors, local or foreign. Consequently, there is a scarcity of directly available funding, which perpetuates underdevelopment, and underdevelopment discourages potential investment. Young nations complain of the lack of interest by foreign investors, but why should foreigners invest their money in a country where the nationals themselves refuse to do so?

In addition, these countries suffer from a social and political environment that is not only unstable but often dangerous. Poverty engenders instability and instability violence. The inability to create an adequate number of stable jobs leads to long-term unemployment and endemic uncertainty. In Iran and Iraq 40 percent of the population is unemployed and nearly all women are excluded from the workforce. Is there anyone who hasn't seen, crossing a village in these countries, rows of idle young men, leaning against a wall like large lizards? With that special humor typical of the disillusioned, they are called *hittites,* literally those who support the wall (from the Arab *hit*). In spite of the revenue from oil production, a third of the Algerian population, especially the young, is unemployed and finds subsistence only through the odd job here and there and by what might be called "street smarts." Is it surprising that there is frequent social turmoil, which is quickly and harshly suppressed? Far from benefiting everyone, even indirectly, this artificial enrichment perversely leads to the impoverishment of the majority of the populace.

THE NEW CITIZEN

The consequences are generally disastrous. They include the emigration of the most talented, the educated, the technicians, who put their talent and skills to work elsewhere. The brain drain is as detrimental as the flight of capital. Economic underdevelopment leads to technological and scientific underdevelopment. Education, now directed toward religion and not sufficiently toward technical training, prevents the formation of a qualified middle class. The gulf between rich and poor gradually grows wider. A tour of Algiers reveals the crumbling structures in the poor quarters, which clash with the handsome buildings inhabited by the nouveaux riches, and previously by Europeans. The absence of a large working class, preventing the formation of a sufficiently robust labor movement, leads to old-fashioned paternalism rather than relative social justice, and to bondage beneath a facade of generosity. Although housemaids today may refuse to call themselves Fatima, insisting they be called Warda or Neila like their bosses, they remain underpaid and at the mercy of their employers. Like some wealthy European almsgiver of centuries past, an employer may boast of sharing a meal with his employees—the annual couscous—or handing out a few gifts at Ramadan, instead of raising their salary and enabling them to eat decently throughout the year. There's nothing wrong with getting rich, as long as it doesn't involve putting pressure on others, yet, in these unfortunate countries, the sheep are pitilessly fleeced, and it's amazing how much can be obtained from sheep that have already been shorn.

For lack of anything better, governments promote folklore, arts and crafts, and tourism. As for tourism, it's better to be a servant than to go hungry. Even in Tunisia, which is often cited as an example for its recent success against poverty, at least a third of its revenue comes from the tourist industry. But these are dead ends. For they perpetuate the artificial character of the economy of these nations and maintain their dependence on the developed world, whose obsequious or rebellious clients they have become, instead of moving toward relative independence, which demands the courage of breaking with established structures and moving resolutely toward the future. Even oil, that divine surprise offered by nature, will not save the third world unless it is used to promote a more diversified economy. The influx of gold brought back by the conquistadores, while providing Spain with apparent prosperity, soon transformed the country into an obese cripple.

Imposters and Potentates

To make such fraud acceptable, imposters are required, capable of imposing this destructive state of affairs through deception or coercion when necessary. The affluent understood this at once and have regularly taken advantage of it. With rare exceptions, third-world countries had, and still have, such men as their leaders: potentates supported by the unseen profiteers of the new regimes. Transparency is certainly not a notable characteristic of these governments. As long as the system functions, these glorified clerks require nothing more than the approval of their hidden supporters. The result is the unusual longevity of the people's ostensible political rulers, which is one of the paradoxes of such countries. With their customary humor, their subjugated populations have pointed out that the only way such rulers leave office is in a coffin. Since they do not derive their authority from the people, they are not subject to the changes of opinion that are characteristic of democracy. So why replace them when they demonstrate their abilities daily and provide all the services expected of them? No coup d'état has

THE NEW CITIZEN

ever prevented such rulers from maintaining order or fostering the acquisition of wealth.

In exchange, aside from the benefits of power itself, even apparent, they obtain, through a mafia-like mechanism of reciprocity, the ability to enrich themselves as well. This explains their obsession with power; the position is too profitable for them to give it up easily. Those close to them profit as well. How many wives, sons, and nephews run profitable companies or benefit indirectly through the intercession of their proxies. As we know, nepotism is one of the specific features of these mafia-like regimes. Those in charge of oil management are nearly always close to the head of state; the ministers of finance, however, rarely have any knowledge of the true revenue stream. By lavishing economic rewards on relatives and friends, these rulers reinforce their own circle of protection. More important, they work hard to establish continuity over time. Pol Pot's son was designated by his father as his immediate successor; in Syria, Asad's son succeeded his father; in Egypt Mubarak has just announced that he has a son. And so it goes. Who would be in a better position to ensure the stability of the regime? If the son fails, a spiritual son, a confidant will serve equally well. Wasn't Mubarak the confidant of Sadat, who was the confidant of Nasser? Morocco has an opportunity to avoid such concerns, since the perpetual sultanate provides for the destiny of the realm.

Like a puppet, the potentate believes he controls his own movements, is invulnerable, eternal. And, while awaiting his distant successor, he will use any means, legal or illegal, to shield his power—primarily by eliminating his pallid competition if they dare show their faces. Police control, violence at the voting booth, phony elections, his success at the polls is so nearly unanimous that foreigners can only smile, while the populace grows enraged. He has at his disposal

THE NEW CITIZEN

the formidable means that the modern world has supplied to contemporary dictators: media, and the technologies for communication, representation, and persuasion, which he will use abundantly, shamelessly. The press is entirely devoted to his apotheosis, but pays a high price. Tightly muzzled, it becomes insipid and colorless, poorly selective, reduced to a handful of constantly repeated topics. One wonders who it actually manages to convince, but it doesn't matter much: any contradictory, and therefore dangerous, information is eliminated and the real truth, that of the nation and the world, is absent, camouflaged, or simply misleading. They say it's worse elsewhere. After all, isn't the global press in the hands of the Jews? The statues of former leaders that dotted the cities of the past appear old-fashioned compared to the modern reproductions in stone, bronze, or oils of the new-world ruler. These outsize effigies, standing or on horseback, dressed in the guise of a civilian or soldier, in traditional costume or a nice three-piece suit, cover all available surfaces. In this systematic enterprise of seduction, television is a providential tool. The ruler's image moves in three dimensions; he walks around, smiles, urges encouragements, soothes his countrymen, right there in the comfort of home. A day doesn't go by when he doesn't show up in everyone's living room, not, as in days gone by, in some stylized portrait hung on the wall, but presiding over a meeting, opening a clinic or religious building, commemorating a national event—present, past, or future. A handful of signs of his prestige, light fixtures along the central avenue, a few megalomaniacal monuments, grandiose but questionable projects, help eradicate the memory of the mud in the streets, the piles of garbage, and the absence of a working sewage system.

THE NEW CITIZEN

Tyrants, Zealots, and Soldiers

No government, no matter how much of a police state, is hermetic, sheltered from inopportune unrest; a fissure may appear through which a molten stream of lava can pass. To endure, the ruler must always be on the alert, redouble his preventive measures, that is, his transformation into a tyrant. Only tyranny, a form of continuous violence, hot or cold, can maintain an oppressive system. So he will multiply the pressure from within and from without. Any journalist that dares allude to him quickly finds himself in prison—a warning to amateurs. To prevent coups he must be wary of everyone, even his closest advisers, his ministers and generals. He must seek alliances among the two other powerful elements in young states: religious zealots and the military, whom he will shower with favors and advantages.

However, the alliance with religious zealots is a game of liar's poker, a zero-sum game. The money men are only interested in money; they would make a deal with the devil if need be. The zealots want everything, bodies and souls. They're not alone either: totalitarian regimes everywhere want to control all aspects of the lives of their citizens. Wearing the veil, for example, is not simply convenient for women or a mode of dress, as is the case with Catholic nuns, it becomes the expression of a more general constraint of femininity, which, once veiled, gloved, enveloped from head to foot, cannot even express itself, must reveal only its eyes. The prohibition against touching a man's hand or of being admired are coercive measures that weigh upon the relations between the sexes. For the veil is a constraint for men as well as women, since it deprives them of any contact with femininity. Similarly, the prohibition against drinking alcohol, of listening to profane music, or looking at images is a way of aggravating

15

THE NEW CITIZEN

desire, of affecting all aspects of lived experience. The ruler knows this, closely monitors his partner/adversary: the rise to power of religious conservatives would lead to complete upheaval and his own ruin. Since no lasting coalition is possible with such individuals, he will sometimes flatter them, sometimes pressure them. But they are always there, waiting for their moment. They can be found in apparently peaceful Morocco, in Egypt, where they are referred to as the "Muslim Brotherhood," even in reserved Tunisia, where it is jokingly said that the fundamentalists only have to shave their beard or hide it in their collar to go unnoticed. In Algeria, where power was nearly cannibalized, the government was forced to make an emergency appeal to a countervailing power group— the military.

The military, which is far from reclusive, has the advantage of being able to impress the crowds with their uniforms, their weapons, their medals, and their theatrical ceremonies. The list of soldiers who have held power in once colonized nations is extensive. The Egyptian Nasser was a colonel, as was Khadafi in Libya. The first president of the Algerian Republic, Ben Bella, was a noncommissioned officer in the French army, and retained the stiffness and bearing of an officer throughout his tenure. He was replaced by Colonel Boumédienne, head of the first true Algerian army, who was later replaced by the current council of generals. Bourguiba in Tunisia was a civilian but, aside from the fact that he assumed complete power toward the end of his life, he was overthrown by a general, Ben Ali, who is still in power. The sultans, the kings of Morocco, have no need to be professional soldiers since they are supported by bellicose Berber tribes. They too held absolute power, accumulating, through a form of divine delegation, the prestige of the sacred and the profane. Argentina's Perón, the darling of nostalgic crowds (in part thanks to his wife's

16

THE NEW CITIZEN

charm), was a colonel. Hugo Chávez, the current president of Venezuela, is a lieutenant colonel. During the 1970s, power was in the hands of military men in Argentina, Brazil, Bolivia, Chile, Uruguay, and the list continues. Civilians who wish to pass themselves off as soldiers engage in self-promotion: they do not resign themselves, as in democratic countries, to being theoretical commanders in chief, they want to command for real. Stalin, the revolutionary, dressed up as a field marshal. He was imitated by Tito, caricatured by Idi Amin of Uganda. They weren't necessarily wrong, for it is more impressive to enter the historical record in military garb. Castro never abandoned his, nor did Mao. Who better than the army, a hierarchical and disciplined organization, obedient by nature, trained to submit without discussion, and to command, could supply such an effective tool to support a despotic regime? In a developing nation stable institutions are rare; the army, like the church, is a kind of state within a state, more highly structured than the actual government. This is true even of Israel, although it is a democracy.

There are risks in this as well. Between the army and the ruler, a different game of liar's poker is played. The army's solidity gives it self-confidence and the desire for a certain degree of autonomy. The tyrant needs the army to survive, the army does not need the tyrant. The military are specialists in the use of force, war is their raison d'être. In a world of violence, they are the most likely to come out on top. How could they avoid the temptation to seize an opportunity to gain political power? The lowliest corporal believes he holds a marshal's baton in his kit bag. Sometimes they find excuses for their ambitions. In such precarious situations, where anything can happen, where steps must be taken to prevent mishaps, only strongmen, men of unquestioned authority, can replace a ruler who is obviously too weak to govern. Any thug capable of leading a few thousands followers, adolescents proud of their Kalashnikovs, can lead an assault against his predecessor.

As a result, what should have been the foundation of a government sheltered from unrest becomes a link in a tragic chain of events. For among those soldiers are sometimes found criminal idiots, who think that force is sufficient to govern a country and who do not blanch at the sight of blood. Such military regimes are not only harsh, they are incompetent, and for that reason frequently overthrown. This is the opposite of democratic states, where power is relatively stable, precisely because it is not imposed but legitimized through a temporary delegation of authority by the people. Military governments collapse as soon as they are challenged by rival leaders, replacing one pseudolegitimate regime with another.

Diversions, Excuses, and Myths

It is easy to understand the prevalence of myth. Director Spike Lee's *Do the Right Thing* makes an observation that has been confirmed for me by a number of friends. An Asian, or an Italian, opens a restaurant in Harlem. He works practically around the clock. The entire family helps out in the store to avoid having to hire extra staff and to save on taxes. The result is that after a while, everyone lives fairly comfortably. The blacks in the neighborhood, who are initially astounded, become furious. They accuse the restaurant owner of taking their money, forgetting that, in return, they received their pizza, shish kebab, or sushi. Following an altercation, they burn the place down. My friends asked me why they didn't do what the Asians or Italians did. My pained response was that these immigrant groups obviously help one another. As

THE NEW CITIZEN

soon as they arrive in the country, they are taken in by their extended family, assisted by various civic associations. Why don't the blacks have their own associations? The explanation given is that this is contrary to their "mentality," that they dislike associations, and so on. When the questioner insists, the real reason is given: "Because they were slaves!" "But," he responds in astonishment, "that was a long time ago."

Black Americans are not a decolonized people, although they have certain traits in common with them, just as they have certain traits in common with the colonized. But their evasive responses are the same. It is the fault of history, it is always the fault of the whites. Dolorism is a natural tendency to exaggerate one's pains and attribute them to another. Like the decolonized, as long as blacks have not freed themselves of dolorism, they will be unable to correctly analyze their condition and act accordingly.

The tyrant will be careful to promote distractions such as these, and partially succeeds. We must not believe that tyrants, civilian or military, are uniformly held in contempt by the people. Like buffalo that follow their leader, even when he leads them into a ravine, human animals display a kind of gregarious mimicry. To the stupefaction of the civilized world, a large majority of Germans, in a nation that was culturally, scientifically, and technically very advanced, followed Adolf Hitler until their defeat. The formerly colonized, socially leaderless, without unions or political leaders, do not have eyes to see or ears to hear. The tyrant, even when he rises to power through the accident of force, discovers that he represents order. Moreover, though they were bloodthirsty dictators, Idi Amin and Saddam Hussein personified resistance to the West; in spite of everything, they were representatives of a new order. Mythmaking can only take root in fertile ground.

The ruler will do his best to convince his citizens that

others are the cause of their problems, not his own machinations, the dysfunctional economy, administrative disorder, or their own shortcomings. If he achieves his objective, the benefit will be twofold: since the sufferings of the decolonized are the persistent result of foreign domination, the decolonized are no longer culpable and the tyrant is let off the hook. The shortcomings, failures, and crimes of the tyrant are determined by an unjust and dark common past. If the decolonized are still not free citizens in a free country, it is because they remain the powerless playthings of some ancient fate. If the economy fails, it's always the fault of the ex-colonizer, not the systematic bloodletting of the economy by the new masters, not the viscosity of their culture, which fails to address its present and the future.

Sometimes this stagnation is attributed to a new ruse of global capitalism, or "neocolonialism," a term sufficiently vague to serve as a screen and rationale. Colonization assumes a colonizing country, colonists, economic exploitation, the control of wealth, direct management, and a captive foreign policy. Colonization involved theft on all levels, but rather than describing it again, it is wiser to examine the present situation, what it has left in its wake. But so-called neocolonialism explains everything and arouses pity. The United States of America, the "great Satan" and cause of all our present woes, has had a tendency to aid in decolonization efforts, not out of any intrinsic goodness but because it felt that direct colonization was outmoded and costly—and possibly because the country was itself once colonized. The United States wants to establish a global system of free exchange to promote the sale of goods. It has been indifferent—and has been reproached for it—to the political regimes of formerly colonized countries and their clients, even when fascists. It went to war in Vietnam, not because the Vietnamese

THE NEW CITIZEN

demanded independence but because, as Communists and the avant-garde of Soviet Russia, they threatened the expansion of free-market economies in Asia. Even in the past, colonization was not responsible for everything. There were famines before colonization; corruption as well. In the Ottoman Empire, which dominated the Arab world for centuries, poorly paid or unpaid civil servants made the conquered populations pay. Although it wasn't its primary purpose, Western colonization did serve as the opportunity for some technical, political, and even cultural advances, as can happen when civilizations come into contact with one another. In many respects, South Africa continues to live off the advances of the past. Although colonization arrested the development of colonized peoples, it did not generate their earlier decline. The decadence of the Arab-Islamic world in particular, after several centuries of expansion and growth, remains one of the mysteries of history. Several reasons have been suggested, and maybe these should be considered collectively. But more simply, every civilization, no matter how brilliant, one day comes to an end. At this point in time it would be more useful to analyze why decolonization has so rarely succeeded. Why, if the colonial tree produced bitter fruit, has the tree of national independence provided us only with stunted and shriveled crops? Why has it still not succeeded in separating the religious from the profane? In freeing critical thinking, the necessary condition for technological and scientific renewal? In relieving the oppression of women? In reforming backward educational systems?

Obviously, nothing comes of nothing; the actual face of the world's young nations bears the imprint of their colonial past along with their own history. In the former French colonies, French is spoken, English in former English colonies, and Portuguese in Brazil. None of which is necessarily bad. Indian and Jordanian officers wear the same tight-fitting beret as their British counterparts and African shock troops wear the beret of the French paratroopers, who borrowed it from the Americans. Clearly, in the jungle of nations, the strong dominate the weak, taking whatever they can take. But this applies to all nations, whether or not they have been colonized. International relations are not governed by pity or philanthropy; another kind of control is at work and needs to be analyzed, but it is not a question of colonization or neocolonization. Colonization has committed enough crimes of its own; it would be pointless to attribute to it those it did not commit.

The world's emerging nations have been independent for fifty years; they have had the time to reform and eliminate, if they really wanted to, the negative sequels of their earlier state of subjection. What forced the members of the Commonwealth to remain together? That's the actual problem: Why haven't these nations found, or tried to find in themselves, the necessary strength to advance? How is it that they can avoid examining their own mistakes? For example, the choice of export crops to the detriment of food crops, the likely cause of famine. The disordered industrialization of Algeria, which nearly ruined the country's agricultural system. Passivity (sometimes even its encouragement) in the face of uncontrolled birthrates for religious reasons and sometimes as a means of putting pressure on the West. Why do they continuously beg for aid from the ex-colonizer? How can a country demand independence and at the same time ask for continued subsidies from the former colonizer? Black Africa continues to solicit the intervention of foreign troops to control internal dissent. The French soldiers who operate in the Ivory Coast did not invade the country, they were called in by the local government. Why didn't they request assistance from another African country?

THE NEW CITIZEN

Some have tried to explain the extreme poverty of the third world similarly as the result of systematic "theft." What does this "theft" signify? To steal means to take someone's goods against their will. Is it really a question of theft? Who has prevented the oil-producing countries from selling their oil at prices they imposed upon the rest of the world, even the most impoverished? In a world governed by competition, the winner takes all. Perhaps, one day, we will manage to establish more humane relations among nations, but for the time being it is a question of neither colonization nor theft. Naturally, this does not excuse the current complacency of the Western powers, if not their complicity with corrupt regimes and their support for the most reactionary of them. For in this way they enable their own domestic industries to thrive and encourage arms purchases, and one can't help but wonder if this isn't another ruse to absorb monetary surpluses.

However, there is little certainty that the capitalist West has an interest in excessively impoverishing the third world. For there would then be far fewer buyers for goods and services and the world would become a more dangerous place. The current situation is already harmful to the world's poorest, but why do young nations resign themselves to this situation? Are the wealthy citizens and leaders of those countries convinced of the need for change? Can we not assume rather that they prefer stasis? That the current situation, in the end, is convenient for them? So little is preordained in these matters that the countries that have made a determined effort to move forward with their development, especially in Asia, are beginning to succeed. The Tunisian exception, even when held back by the incomprehensible police pressure found there, proves that anything is possible. Illiteracy has nearly disappeared, the condition of women has improved substantially. But here too aren't we ignoring the real reasons for poverty, which are internal and, therefore, susceptible to change? Namely, that the wealthy and the rulers want to distract the attention of the people, convince them that their poverty is inevitable, the result of fate or some foreign plot, hoping to disarm resentment and prevent revolt.

A Convenient Conflict

The Israeli–Palestinian conflict is, in this sense, typical. A solution could have been found years ago if the parties were not so embedded in their respective mythologies. Clearly, the Palestinians are dominated by the Israelis and the conflict will not go away so long as this situation prevails. No people has the right to dominate another, and cannot succeed in doing so forever. Jewish nationalists, Zionists, had a dream of creating a Jewish state throughout all of Palestine. No doubt, they need to abandon that idea as well as the territories where the Palestinians are in the majority; either that or resign themselves to a state of continuous terrorism and continuous war, a condition liable to lead to their own disappearance—which the entire Arab world would very much like to see. A negotiated solution to establish two states, no matter how mediocre this may appear to both sides, would be beneficial for everyone, Palestinians and Israelis, Arabs and Jews. For the conflict extends beyond the Palestinians and Israelis, involving nearly all the Arab-Muslim countries and the majority of the world's Jews. The Palestinians are not as isolated as they claim; they are the foot soldiers of the Arab world, which flatters them as it leads them to the slaughter. They have the financial and political support of twenty-two Arab nations, which supply them with weapons, money, and tactical support. A few years back, Arab diplomacy managed to put up for a vote at the United Nations a motion condemning Zionism as a form of racism. The Arab world being what it is, it is far from certain that the foundation of a Jewish state in a region that is considered to be their exclusive domain was such a good idea. They have not accepted it until now and no one can predict when they will, or even if they will.

Israel, however, is not a colonial settlement, which would therefore be legitimate to destroy, an idea the Arab states have tried to promulgate. Aside from its domination of the Palestinians, which is unacceptable, it has none of the characteristics of such a state. Nor is it a product of the Crusades, a religious excrescence of Europe, destined sooner or later to vanish off the map from Christianity's lassitude. Like Palestine for the Palestinians, Israel is a national fact, the response to an untenable condition and a collective desire, with its own imaginary, binding it, rightly or wrongly, to this earth. This is how the United Nations viewed the situation when it determined the constitutions of the two sovereign states. However, to threaten the destruction of Israel would have catastrophic consequences. With its back to the wall, the country would defend itself, and its destruction would exact a terrible price from everyone involved. Is its obliteration worth such a cost? We must also consider the indelible shame of the Arab states, for such an act would recall the Nazi genocide in the history of modern Germany and the Armenian genocide in the history of Turkey.

When seen in its proper context, compared to the magnitude of the problems—demographic, economic, political, social, cultural, and religious—that now face the Arab world, the Israeli–Palestinian conflict turns out to be a minor drama in a small corner of the world, just one among many. Obviously, the misfortune of the Arabs does not arise from the existence of Israel; even if the country didn't exist, none of these problems would be resolved. On the contrary,

THE NEW CITIZEN

an accurate evaluation of the Israeli–Palestinian conflict and its peaceful resolution would be a sign of renewed health. In fact, it is a rather ordinary struggle between two small emerging nations, whose national claims unfortunately turned out to involve a territorial conflict. The last Palestinian revolt, the second Intifada, which drew significant media attention, cost two thousand lives. That's two thousand too many. But a quick glance at any collection of newspapers will show that, in the past few decades alone, there have been more than a million deaths in Biafra, five hundred thousand in Rwanda, uncounted massacres in Uganda and the Congo, three hundred thousand deaths in Burundi, two hundred thousand victims in Colombia since 1964 along with three million displaced persons, the eradication of Communists in Indonesia, estimated at five hundred thousand, and the terrifying massacres of the Khmer by their own people. To focus on the Arab world itself, how many lives did decolonization cost in Algeria and France? Five hundred thousand Algerians died, according to the French, a million according to the Algerians; seventy thousand young French soldiers lost their lives. The small war between the two Algerian liberation movements, the FLN (Front de libération nationale) and Messali Hadj's MNA (Mouvement national algérien), cost ten thousand lives. The victorious FLN massacred at least fifty thousand *harkis*. We do not know how many died in the wars between Egypt and Libya, between Algeria and Morocco, between Chad and Libya. How many people had their throats slit or were gunned down by Algerian fundamentalists or as a result of army reprisals? In Iraq, Hussein gassed tens of thousands of his people. And what about the million Armenians assassinated by the Turks? The Russian pogroms? The numbers in this sinister arithmetic grow larger by the day. During a riot in Bombay over the placement of a mosque, the

26

THE NEW CITIZEN

Indians, citizens of what is supposedly the largest democracy in the world and the most tolerant, massacred two thousand Muslims; the equivalent in two days of two years of the Intifada. Considered in its entirety, the third world has never stopped being the theater of horrible tribal wars, ethnic and national.

One of many myths is that if the Arabs were to unify they would become a power comparable to if not greater than their former empires. Egypt's Nasser used this argument for his own purposes: oil and Arab demographics would enable him to achieve political power ("We'll win with the wombs of our women!"). But unbridled growth is one of the plagues of the Arab world, whose revenues are regularly unable to cope with the rising tide of population. If the resources from oil sales were used to benefit these countless masses, the situation would change completely. Moreover, the Arabs have space and geography at their disposal. But money from oil sales can also be used to purchase weapons and sometimes men, even in the heart of the Western world, as recent scandals have demonstrated. Libya's Khadafi wanted to be Nasser's successor, but Nasser died too young to know if his dream could be realized. Saddam Hussein became a hero of the Arab crowds. In the suburbs of Paris, in Ramallah in Palestine, and Amman, Jordan, they cried out, "We are all Saddam!" Naturally, the wealthy would have to contribute to this movement and the communal action, but in dreams everything is permitted; and if need be, force could be used. This remains one of Osama bin Laden's objectives, a man who uses terror, as much against the West as to provoke the collapse of the Arab regimes that resist his grandiose project.

The second myth, correlative with the first, is that the state of Israel is a thorn, a cancerous growth in the body of the Arab nation, which prevents this unification. The destruction of

27

THE NEW CITIZEN

Israel would thus be a preliminary condition for this strategy of unification.

Until now the Arab nations have failed in this twofold task. The interminable Israeli–Palestinian conflict is the proof of this failure, and the scope of their disappointment is understandable. They will not rest until they overcome it, by maintaining a state of conflict if need be. Only once did they come close to succeeding. This was during the Yom Kippur War, when the existence of the Jewish state, surrounded on all sides, cut in two by several Arab armies, was genuinely threatened. But in the end Israel managed to extricate itself, though the Arab leaders had benefited from the technical and military assistance of Soviet advisers in Egyptian uniforms. Nonetheless, the Arabs continue to make preparations, materially and psychologically, for this decisive struggle. When war failed they had recourse to diplomatic pressure and terrorism. Boycotts, attacks, hidden financing for terrorists, ongoing battles in international organizations, in academic, cultural, scientific, and sports organizations, the reprinting and mass distribution of anti-Semitic literature, such as the famous *Protocols of the Elders of Zion,* the cultivation of a systematic culture of hatred among the public and throughout the educational curriculum. To create human time bombs, they held Palestinian refugees in camps, where they didn't even have the right to build permanent housing; otherwise they would long ago have been integrated into the Arab host countries, something that had to be prevented at any cost. There is no mystery to the Arab texts used for domestic consumption; they openly discuss the destruction of Israel. Didn't the first president of the Algerian republic, Ben Bella, go so far as to declare that, if he had had an atomic bomb, he would have launched it against Israel, which had become a kind of absolute evil? To speak of Israel in terms other than as

28

THE NEW CITIZEN

a historical, even metaphysical, disease that the Arab world needed to be cleansed of became a form of blasphemy that had to be punished. Giving it a place on a map was a sacrilege, a felony. As if, by denying its existence, it could magically be made to disappear. This effort was facilitated by the fact that the Jews served as an excellent scapegoat for the problems of others. Israel's existence was far too convenient. "Try to understand what I'm saying," confided an Arab student on the radio, making a kind of desperate avowal. "I have been raised since birth in this atmosphere, where conflict with the Zionists was fundamental. Its resolution must occur before that of any other conflict; because it is the source of all our sorrows. And you ask me to put it in perspective! I've tried several times, but have never managed to do so."

The effort has been successful, but at what price? The confusion of the young, control of intellectuals, the channeling of Arab opinion into this one area, diverting attention away from every other problem. The Palestinian question and support of religious fundamentalism throughout the world, both financed by Saudi Arabia, contribute to the stability of the kingdom. But it is a pyrrhic victory. The result has been stagnation in every field of life, the sidetracking of human endeavor toward the support of a myth. The recourse to myth, though it may help make life bearable, rarely comes without a price. At the very least it distances one from reality. But isn't this what the rich and powerful want? The Palestinian question, legitimate but minor, has become symbolically disproportionate. It is part of the trap developed by the privileged to maintain their people in a state of subjection and confusion.

The 2002 UN report on the region notes the failure of development in the Arab world. That same year, in July, again at the UN's request, Arab specialists, working together on a

29

committee, drafted a report on the state of the Arab-Muslim world. After listing the problems, they went on to denounce the instrumentalization of the Israeli–Palestinian conflict to divert attention from the search for effective solutions. In 2003 another report concluded not only that there was continued stagnation, but that the situation in the Arab world as a whole had grown worse. Under pressure from Arab diplomats, these reports remain confidential.

The Failure of the Intellectuals

Third-world intellectuals have also failed their societies. However, you didn't need to be an expert to perceive the obvious, only courage. Yet, with rare exceptions, this was the one thing lacking. On the contrary, intellectuals seem to be afflicted by the same paralysis of thought and action that has affected everyone else. The most common excuse was that of solidarity. One shouldn't overwhelm one's fellow citizens when they are living in such misery. That would be like supporting their enemies. We can see how, not fully recovered from their earlier subjection, of which they retained the still painful wounds, any criticism, even though justified, might lead them to suspect foul play, a reflection of the aggression of the colonizers, triggering a wave of uncontrollable emotion.

But by giving in, intellectuals have abandoned their specific function, which is to fairly evaluate society's needs, the necessary first step to positive change. Wasn't it this critical thinking, conducted by Western thinkers, that freed modern society from obscurantist leaders, gave it its dynamism and creativity, the source of all progress? When Islamic civilization was at its height, its intellectuals benefited from additional freedoms. Today, there is really nothing equivalent to an Omar Khayyám, who had the sacrilegious audacity to praise wine and women, even displaying a discreet sense of irony toward religious subjects.

It's not the same—and this is still true today—to be an intellectual on the shores of the Seine or in Tehran, Damascus, or Algiers. The risks are not the same: the potential for immediate accusations of treason, or even blasphemy, leads to caution. A contemporary example is Salman Rushdie, who for years was forced to lead a clandestine existence, expecting every day to be his last. The first time a book on atheism appeared in the Arab world, its author, Professor Sadok el Azem, was forced out of the University of Beirut. But, even as refugees in large European cities, Arab intellectuals have continued to remain silent, as if they had interiorized the proscriptions of their home community. One of the best known among them, the Arab-American, Edward Said, a Christian, went so far as to accuse them of cowardice. If danger can paralyze each of them individually, why have they not come together to offer some form of collective denunciation?

For some time now, the acceleration of history and its increasingly urgent challenges, the now overt Islamist demands, the violence, the reaction of the West, the war against the Taliban and the ambiguities of the Iraq war, the continued rigidity of tyranny, the stagnation, if not the regression, of social behaviors, possibly also some embarrassment in the face of the questioning glances of their European counterparts, seem to have troubled some of these intellectuals sufficiently to cause them to venture outside their reservation. A shudder of life has finally taken shape on the surface of their apparent immobility. It is encouraging that in Paris a handful of lay Muslim associations have been established. But for the most part, they have done nothing but offer apologias, pleadings to defend their own members, rather than manifest any genuine signs of assertiveness, whenever they are asked to

THE NEW CITIZEN

stand up for their claims. Telling the truth to one's people, even if others can hear it and make use of it, does not add to their misery but, on the contrary, is a sign of respect and assistance. The bad faith of groups is more damaging than that of individuals; it is essential, therefore, that their more farsighted and courageous members attempt to enlighten them. If no one is willing to take the trouble to do this, then those groups can only look forward to a loss of credibility and authority.

To restore some sense of balance Arab-Muslim intellectuals would have to make use of a tradition other than the submission to dogma and power, of siding with opinion. However, there no longer exists, if there ever did in the Arab-Muslim world, that great public tribunal characteristic of democracy, where everyone can publicly give his opinion without unnecessary risk. True controversies are rare, except possibly for unimportant details, where disagreements occur against a background of underlying unity. As a result, any condemnation of wrongdoing and scandal always comes from the exterior, from those outside the community, leading to suspicions of bias or perversity. Therefore, until now little has been said about the stupefying phenomenon of suicide attacks, which presents both political and moral problems. We should not expect them to be necessarily for or against, but that they openly address the question, even if they disagree among themselves. Hardly a word about the condition of women is heard. Not a single statement about the fate of minorities, some of whose members have contributed to the independence of their country at the risk of their life; not a sign of recognition. On the contrary, they most often find themselves being gradually eliminated from the country's civil-service bureaucracy. In this way a great occasion is lost to build, at least in words, an open and multicultural nation, one

THE NEW CITIZEN

that includes the Algerian Kabyles, the Egyptian Copts, Jews and Christians . . . precisely what intellectuals living in the West demand for themselves in their host countries! Almost no one openly opposed the Taliban regime, or they did so with such ambiguous arguments that one has to wonder if these weren't a form of veiled approval. No one dared to condemn, unless in private, Saddam Hussein or supported the necessity of putting the dictator in such a position that he was no longer able to harm anyone. Nearly everyone had an opinion about Israel's right to exist, even when mixed with condemnations. Among the Arab public we know that virulent anti-semitism is rampant. To the extent that they believe that the United States is acting against Arab interests, such unanimity is easy to understand; but isn't it astonishing that there are no discordant voices, even if they are wrong?

There was always a kind of unanimous silence, embarrassment. There are casuists who attempt to find in the Koran and its interpreters ways to justify the unjustifiable, deliberately forgetting its contradictory passages. Apologist historians go out of their way to learnedly explain that what can be criticized today in Islam are merely the remnants of an anti-Islamic period, overlooking the fact that we might have done away with such remnants since then. Why, for example, has the condition of women not changed? Why have they not abolished the status of the *dhimi,* a protected foreigner not entitled to citizenship, never equal to the Muslim before the law? Hypocrisy abounds. There are those who display their obedience but rarely give it a second thought, condemning the use of alcohol in public and drinking at home with friends; those who practice a kind of two-sided language, being democratic and tolerant abroad but becoming obedient children once they've returned to their native soil; there are fanatics disguised as democrats; opportunists who approve

33

THE NEW CITIZEN

of power in exchange for a place in its shadow. The greatest number, those who are intentionally silent, the autistic, who have lost the use of their ears, their eyes, and their speech, have become unwitting accomplices through their tacit approval. Yet how much effort needs to be expended to demonstrate that "Islam is compatible with human rights," that there exists a "moderate Islam," tolerant, nonviolent, and even, depending on the period, humanist and universalist? This would be easy enough to do with a handful of quotes stressing tolerance, and by avoiding those that highlight exclusion and violence. By forgetting that Muhammad was also a leader of warriors, who shared his plunder with his troops, and that his succession was an occasion for massacre; that Islam was conquering not only in words but also in war, as Christianity had been for centuries. In more general terms, why demand that texts—texts that are no doubt interesting and have made their mark upon society—provide more than they can give, unless it is to continue to promote some veiled apology? These texts should be placed on a shelf, along with the religious books of other religions, as a contribution to the history of world literature. This is not to attack Islam; all religions are intolerant, exclusive, restrictive, and sometimes violent. The conception of a "moderate Islam," which some willingly defend, is misguided: there is no such thing as a moderate religion, even though there are more or less faithful believers, more or less respectful of its dogmas and rites, believers who, for that matter, also arouse the wrath and irony of fundamentalists.

The only thing missing from this picture is the strong-minded individual, frankly atheist or, to put it more prudently, agnostic. Such individuals have been a part of the history of Islam, even though they sometimes paid with their lives. Are there no independent minds in the vast Muslim

THE NEW CITIZEN

world? Is there no one who will play the part of Voltaire or Nietzsche and criticize traditional thinkers, or even—horror of horrors!—Holy Scripture, openly and not so indirectly as to lead one to wonder about what his or her real ideas might be? It is highly likely that such ideas are expressed in private. But while the fundamentalists—we must recognize their courage—assert their retrograde convictions and announce that, sooner or later, using violence or murder if necessary, they will impose them on everyone, the intellectuals continue to remain silent, terrorized by the threats of the fundamentalists, the screams of the crowds, and the unrelenting hold of religious law, the sharia. It is true that in Muslim countries any suspected apostasy is often punished with death, legal if not actual. As recently as 2002 there were Egyptian magistrates who were ready to jail, torture, and condemn fifty homosexuals. Those who denied any criminal activity were required to submit to a ludicrous "certificate of anal virginity." In their defense there was no petition by Arab intellectuals, nor by any others, for that matter. Another court ordered that a legitimate couple, two people who loved one another, be separated because one of the two was held to hold perverse opinions. If all Arab-Muslim agnostics would lend a helping hand, the fundamentalists would retreat and the Arab world would be transformed. But they are terrified by the threat of excommunication, which would cast doubt on their identity. "You are not a *true* Muslim" was until recently considered a dangerous insult. Intellectuals overlook the fact that in acting as they do, they have abandoned to the fundamentalists the right to define what a Muslim is. Doesn't this make them resigned accomplices of their accusers? It is not up to fundamentalists to determine who is and who isn't a Muslim. Moreover, being a Muslim isn't a question of dogmatic definition but, as the condition of Jews or Gypsies attests, an objective

35

THE NEW CITIZEN

condition, which, relatively speaking, escapes the control of definer and defined.

In spite of their docility, they continue to be regarded with suspicion by opinion and power, like all intellectuals, which is to their credit but also overstates their influence. Just as if we believed that the French Revolution was triggered by Voltaire and Rousseau, instead of looking for the causes in the injustice and paralysis of the French ancien régime.

Fiction and Reality

If philosophical and political debate has become sterile because it is muzzled or subservient, what about literature? Writers have a marvelous tool at their disposal, imagination, which allows them to make believe. They can attribute to fictional characters things they themselves feel and think. Fifty novels from a given period provide a richer source of insight than tons of newsprint published during the reign of a dictator. Balzac and Maupassant do a better job of reflecting their epoch, its dramas and social milieu, than the conformist analysts of the same period. The writer is a storyteller, but often, also, an accuser. What does the literature of the ex-colonized tell us?

Paradoxically, it's harder to be a writer in the postcolonial period than during colonization. Before, the decolonized wrote in the language of the colonizer, the only language he knew well, even when directed against the colonizer. By denouncing, directly or indirectly, colonization, its fundamental injustice, its petty daily miseries, the oppressive and humiliating presence of a foreign police and army, economic exploitation, political frustration, and cultural repression, he contributed with his pen to the rebellion of his fellow countrymen. Because he expressed himself in the language of the

THE NEW CITIZEN

oppressor he could, it is true, only be understood by them; but he was at the same time able to act, although in a limited way, by affecting public opinion.

But now, not having learned any other, the writer should use this same language to examine his own society. Continuing to ply his craft, he should depict the incompetence, the egotism, the profitable complicity of the ruling classes, the pressures from his own government. But what is referred to as an independent thinker, exercising a critical intellect directed toward his peers, still doesn't exist in the new society. With the exception of the plastic arts and music, whose language is inaudible to the majority, all writing is suspect and controlled. The only writing that is tolerated is conformist, the praise of politicians and religious leaders, bland folkloric tales, reminders of a supposedly glorious past that will help the people forget the mediocrity of the present. The writer can only "suggest," describing some imaginary country, or make use of symbolist rhetoric; beyond this he shares the unmitigated silence of the intellectuals. There was not much to be heard from black writers, or intellectuals for that matter, during the genocides in Biafra, Uganda, and the Sudan. Nor did we hear much from Maghrebi intellectuals during the absurd, bloody conflicts between neighboring countries or during the liquidation of minorities. The massacres of the Kurds by the Iraqis also failed to impress Iraqi writers and intellectuals, even those in exile, just as Turkish intellectuals remained silent about the suffering of the Armenians.

How is it that they have been able to remain silent while arbitrariness, corruption, and crime flourish around them? Certainly there are risks — writers have always been a significant portion of the prison population, a very significant one if journalists are included. But there is the question of their own resistance. They felt it was an insult to their communities to

37

insist on the persistent famines that caused an increase in poverty in and around cities, or the rising homeless population, or the growing number of those collected every morning on the sidewalks of Indian or Latin American cities who had died from hunger or cold during the night. Like every male, they were ambiguous about women's sexuality and continued servitude, one of the plagues of the Arab-Muslim world and one of the causes of its stasis. They have still not been able to reconsider the role of religion in Islamic civic life, and they dare not assert its necessary separation from politics. They continue to confuse, or pretend to confuse, faith and social and historical belonging, as if it were impossible to be a non-Muslim Arab; some of us suffered from this. It is remarkable that today women writers are more numerous and freer than men writers in the Maghreb and throughout the third world. That is because they have everything to gain from speaking out and look forward to a change in attitudes.

Assuming that the writer has the fortitude or the wiles (this explains the abundance of pseudonyms), which literature fortunately supplies in abundance, to bear witness in spite of everything, and that the censors close their eyes, pretending this is no more than a fanciful invention by an irresponsible artist (the censors can read between the lines and have their own agents), the writer will confront a second difficulty: the absent reader.

Between the writer and the longed-for reader arises an unforeseen obstacle: in what language must he write to be understood? His hesitation regarding the final choice of a common language, between the inherited language of the colonizers and the national language, the uncertain needs of education, the missteps and weakness of local publishers, even when supported by the government (for which they are monitored and kept in check), hardly favor the birth of a

THE NEW CITIZEN

mature reading public, any more than they do of independent authors. From time to time, to put an end to this linguistic anguish and affirm the exclusivity of traditional language, a government may decide to forcibly use Arabic in schools, government offices, even on signs in stores. There was a time when French was ostracized, when the former students of French lycées were refused jobs and French speakers were singled out as being bad citizens, almost traitors. This led to the belief, for myself as well as others, that writing in French was nearing its end—about which we were fortunately wrong. The same held true for all languages other than Arabic. The current Algerian president once proclaimed that "Kabyle will become an official language over my dead body!" And Kabyle first names are still unlawful in Algeria. Yet, aside from the complications thus introduced into everyday life, which continues to be thoroughly impregnated by the language of the colonizer, a nation's language cannot be decided by ukase. Who would understand a speech in purely classical Arabic? Even the choice of Arabic is not without complications. Which version should be spoken? One's mother tongue or that of the streets? The language of the press and the media? Or that of the Koran, an atemporal decree, which cannot keep pace with a language in constant evolution, one that follows its own path through time, the twists and turns of daily life, to the point that it becomes nearly unrecognizable? How many contemporary French speakers can read Rabelais or Montaigne without difficulty? While any prognostication would be arbitrary, it is likely, in spite of the resistance of traditionalists (who are even opposed to vowelization because Koranic Arabic does not use it), that the language of the Koran will, notwithstanding the efforts toward scholarly unification, one day become as uncommon as Latin. The desire to freeze a language once and for all is a utopian dream since the reality it

39

THE NEW CITIZEN

expresses is not fixed. In any event, the true writer does not write in a sacred language because he reinvents his own. Any imposed language is a stilted language, which leads to the use of rhetoric, stress, and symbolism. This is still largely true of classical Arabic, which remains a sacred language, enclosed in the shackles of the Koran.

So should the writer use the language of the colonizer? In doing so he will continue to speak principally to expatriates, from whom he expects consecration in the literary pantheon. This is a drama common to all Francophone writers, who are as terrorized by Paris as non-Parisian writers living in France. Moreover, experiencing a vague feeling of betrayal, the decolonized writer will twist and squirm to apologize. He will claim, for example, that he has appropriated, violated, destroyed the language of the colonizer, along with other witless comments, as if all writers didn't do the same. For the simple truth is that, for the present and possibly the distant future as well, it is the only tool he will have mastered and without it he would be reduced to silence. No doubt language is part of collective personality, of which it serves as a binder, but it is also a tool for communication. But the best tool for communication remains the language of the foreigner. This was already true during the period of colonization, and it is still true now. Was it worth so much effort only to face the same dilemma all over again?

Cultural Lethargy

The shortcomings of intellectuals, whether characterized as resignation or betrayal, play a part in national cultural lethargy, even though it can be partly justified and merely reflects a more general problem. For it leaves the field open for those who opt for mystic effusion in place of rationality, the strait-

THE NEW CITIZEN

jacket of strict membership to the openness of universalism; to those who, in place of a depressing or humiliating present, can dream only of a return to a golden age, a renewed fusion, the only productive kind in their view, of religion, culture, and politics, where the splendors of the past will flourish again in some new Andalusia, a renascent caliphate similar to that of Baghdad, where tolerance, justice, and prosperity will reign. They forget that, in those so-called earthly paradises, there were dominated minorities, toward whom they displayed what could at best be described as condescending benevolence. But we can no more turn back the historical clock than we can climb back into our mother's womb.

Culture is a kind of curio shop, where each of us can pick and choose according to our desires and fears, where the best and the worst coexist side by side, personal fantasies and critical intellect, old, worn-out recipes and the rush of individual genius. We devise new solutions—technological or reassuring—that challenge nature and history, the difficulties of life in common, the unknown within us and around us. We also discover harmonies that simplify our lives, art, philosophy, law, and morals, along with our most questionable desires, our prejudice and greed, our compensatory representations, our derisive use of magic and superstition, our religious expectations. We should not be surprised, then, if the ruler and his servants are suspicious of the first aspect of culture and privilege the second, which is put to use in the work of persuasion and cohesion both for himself and for those in power. But in doing so the ruler destroys any vague impulse toward renewal before it has had a chance to mature.

Living culture is an ongoing questioning of traditional beliefs—testing and adapting them to the inevitable transformation all societies undergo. It is thus inherently dangerous, iconoclastic and heretical, because it needs to free itself of all

THE NEW CITIZEN

restraints in order to breathe freely. Faced with these tentative steps, the ruler will, on the contrary, support the most fossilized aspects of tradition. He will exhume and honor, as if he were a contemporary, some medieval thinker like Averroës, who will receive more honors than when he was alive, pretending to forget that during his lifetime the philosopher was viewed suspiciously for what was most innovative in his work. But centuries have passed since then. Those venerable thinkers, whatever their merit in their own lifetime, are incapable of addressing today's problems. The ruler will then resuscitate some antique hero, now become the—contradictory—symbol of a prestigious past and a bright future, overlooking the fact that his hero was frequently at odds with the most conservative of his contemporaries. After having burned Joan of Arc, they made her a saint and gathered her ashes to place in reliquaries. The ruler will promote the most outdated elements of national folklore, as was done during colonization—the fantasias with their rusty blunderbusses, regional parades in traditional costumes, preceded by fanfares and littered with pennants glorifying local saints. He will flatter ethnic and national myths. He will invent others if necessary, which require everyone to make the supreme sacrifice. He will suggest that he himself is the reincarnation of the great men of the past, like Saladin, sent from heaven for the great task to which he is destined.

No doubt a reminder of the glories of a past (assuming it was glorious) otherwise obscured by colonization is not without value. It initially restores a sense of pride to an aspiring people; it strengthens a collective identity shaken by decades of foreign domination. The rebirth of a national language, for example, is one such affirmation of the collective ego. But language should not only express the singular soul of the nation but also respond to everyday needs, national and

THE NEW CITIZEN

international. Years of lethargy, however, have turned it into an instrument that is, at least momentarily, culturally and technologically unsuitable. It is still incapable of mastering a full-blown culture, that is, one that is innovative and inventive. Therefore, continued use will be made of the language of the ex-colonizer. Certainly, it has been more convenient, until now, to speak English or French, than Arabic or Hindi. At times the distribution of local languages is such that, in the end, none of them is privileged. There is a sense of resignation in seeing the triumph of the language of the ex-colonizer, the only thing shared among the various ethnicities. So, Portuguese is the official language of all the inhabitants of Brazil, its former colony, including its writers. In North Africa, for years it was more common to hear French than Arabic in ministerial meetings, since the ministers, for the most part the products of bourgeois elites, spoke French better than Arabic. Attempts at systematic use of Arabic have been so alarmingly bad that it was necessary to take a step backward. Paradoxically, the impact of the ex-colonizer's culture has never been so great because of new publics who often speak the foreigner's language better than their own. We also need to consider the growing influence of television and radio. Technology is still French in this part of the world.

Culture is also a bond, a social cement, a communal site, a refuge from the wretchedness of existence, a beacon and escape valve. But this exclusive anchorage—to a reconstructed past or the splendors of a hypothetical future, the excessive valuation placed on the past and unreasonable expectations for the future, navigation between phantoms and myths, an archaic golden age and a glorious future—leads to the same result: the destruction of the present. Isn't this what the aristocrats want? Instead of helping to free people's intellects and allowing them to flourish, pseudoculture has misled them

THE NEW CITIZEN

about the nature of true culture. However, participation in the new world, which is now incumbent upon everyone, requires immediate answers.

Even though it is painful to admit, the progress acquired by the West is often more appropriate than traditional solutions. The situation is not one in which, as has been repeated so complacently, several civilizations clash. There is now a single, global, civilization that affects everyone, including fundamentalists, who seem to have no qualms about using cell phones, the Internet, the banking system, automobiles, and planes, and may one day just as easily embrace rockets and sophisticated weapons—technologies they did not invent. It is far from clear that they are entirely sincere in claiming to defend values that have become increasingly unsustainable. Wouldn't this imply that they are trying, rather, to maintain their grip on the attention of the populace? The real challenge everyone faces right now is to provide all the inhabitants of the planet with the healthiest and most comfortable life possible through the management of natural resources, without the need for deadly confrontations and upheavals. Some believe that stasis will be the best guarantee of privilege but, under the visible layer of snow, those countries are volcanoes waiting to erupt.

The Clerics' Plot

Should we be surprised that religion has been used systematically and tirelessly for political purposes throughout the world? The ruler grants his servants whatever favors or benefits they desire in exchange for their control over the populace. There is a sharp contrast between the resigned misery of the population, sustained by this ongoing call to submission, and the glorious presence of religion—the mosques

THE NEW CITIZEN

that punctuate the landscape, the minarets that dot the sky, the voice, now amplified by loudspeakers, of the muezzins heard throughout the day. The new masters build more madrasas than schools. In Morocco, 50 percent of the population is illiterate, but the previous sultan constructed "the greatest mosque in the contemporary Muslim world." The very Catholic head of state in the Ivory Coast, Houphouët-Boigny, ordered the "greatest modern cathedral" to be built, a gesture redolent of the European Middle Ages, when the splendor of religious construction contrasted with the misery of the parishioners. Even Tunisia did not fail to write into article 1 of its constitution that it was a Muslim state. Too bad for the minorities. Bourguiba, a social democrat on the French model and probably a freemason, had initially decided to break the hold of the "enturbannés," the turban heads—this is the term he used. But after a number of his rodomontades, including the famous episode of the glass of orangeade (certainly no alcohol!) he drank during a televised speech ("You would do better," he exclaimed to his stunned compatriots, "to devote your energy to developing the country than to weaken yourselves by fasting for the entire month of Ramadan!"), he backed away from the immensity of the task before him. Bourguibism was an unexpected opportunity for Tunisia and a possible model for the Arab world, but Bourguiba was no more than a flash in the pan, the resistance too strong. He subsequently proceeded to scatter mosques across the countryside. Being a cautious administrator, he understood that a persistent conflict with the clerics would have been dangerous for his rule; but it did him no good, for in the end they got the better of him. His successor, Ben Ali, remembered the lesson. Although he kept the fundamentalists under a watchful eye, he stopped persecuting them. He did not go so far as to recommend that women again begin wearing a veil and men a beard, he simply asked for a certain amount of discretion. Saudi Arabia lavishly funded the construction of mosques throughout the world, but no funds were given to a school or university unless it was religious and medieval, no clinic was built unless attached to a mosque, for which it served as a kind of waiting room.

Why should a ruler, even a lay ruler, deprive himself of such a convenient crutch? Why should Saudi Arabia, pickled in its billions of dollars managed for the exclusive profit of a clan, desire change? Doesn't it also oversee the fabled and lucrative pilgrimage to Mecca? Modern education would risk disturbing the people's intellect and might lead them to look elsewhere. But God, unchangeable in essence, does not like revolution, and the Saudi leaders, like the sultan of Morocco, "Commander of the Faithful," are in the service of God, just as the Iraqi government or the Turkish government, which claim to be lay governments. On the contrary, it is too tempting to excite religious passions in times of crisis. Hindu India and Muslim Pakistan both appealed to their homegrown religious fanatics to defend their policies. During the first Iraq war, the American leader and the Iraqi leader rivaled one another in calling upon divine assistance. Obviously it is better for God to be with you than against you. We can take advantage of his help to crush the liberals.

But there is a price for everything. If you raise a baby crocodile in your apartment, one day he will eat you. The Americans gave aid to the Taliban in fighting the Russians and later went to war with them. The Israelis initially encouraged the Palestinian fundamentalists in Hamas, who then turned against them. The ruler knows this; he knows that if the fundamentalists gain power, he will be eliminated. To avoid this he will practice a balancing act, sometimes granting them favors,

THE NEW CITIZEN

sometimes tightening the screws. The Islamic veil, the beard, the mosques, the confraternities serve as escape valves, but all the Arab governments know they are raising crocodiles in their midst. This providential aid, granted through the intermediary of the priests, is not disinterested. It is a poisoned alliance, where everyone, using his own weapons, tries to neutralize, then despoil, the others.

The ultimate goal of the fundamentalists has always been the creation of an Islamic state, where power would be concentrated in their hands. And in this overt struggle they are far from being the weakest player. Given the absence of other cohesive forces in still fragile nations, religion continues to be one of the foundations of a shared identity. It retains a tenacious hold on intellect and behavior; it is a relatively coherent system; it contains beliefs, rituals, and morality, which reinforce one another and combine to incorporate all aspects of life, individual and collective. It affects all social, economic, and cultural functions. Why would it turn its back on political power? To accomplish this would have required relaxing religion's grasp on the layperson, at least in institutional environments. Europe has been working toward this for several centuries, the Islamic world has yet to begin.

In the meantime, the ruler makes use of this merger of politics and religion, even if navigating between them is difficult. He plays out the line to the fundamentalists, but holds the rod firmly. Assembling for Friday prayer is authorized by governments, even encouraged in all the Muslim countries. These assemblies are a pressure cooker of sorts, where furious imams express and assuage, in language of astonishing violence for religious sermons, the frustrations, the anger, and the demands of the faithful. But the mosques are crawling with police spies, who enable their governments to evaluate

THE NEW CITIZEN

the temperature of the crowd on a regular basis. If there is any risk of danger, the necessary steps are taken.

At times, however, history escapes the control of the ruler and the ulemas carry the day. It is far from obvious that if elections, genuinely free elections, were to be held throughout the Arab world, the fundamentalists wouldn't win. This was the case in Algeria, where the army succeeded—just barely—in neutralizing the fundamentalists' power, even though it was legitimately won at the ballot box. Kemal's Turkey has functioned with an Islamist government. Iran, after making overtures toward a very modern form of liberalism, suddenly made an about-face toward the shadows of medievalism. At the same time, a variety of methods are used to make new converts for Islam: constant and underhanded agitation, the clever use of cultural and social services, clinics and family assistance, a strategy of conversion, even in mixed marriages, which are easier to arrange in Islamic countries than anywhere else, the promise of a radiant hereafter contrasted with the misery of everyday life.

But the victory of the fundamentalists would be a step backward; none of the problems that threaten the modern world would be resolved. On the contrary, it would be a systematic return to the past, involving the exclusive use of traditional texts, suspicion of all novelty and critical thought, the restriction, if not suppression, of the majority of civil liberties, greater police surveillance than that experienced under lay rulers, increased attacks on women, the rigorous separation of the sexes, the stifling of the most anodyne and most natural aspirations of the young—music, dancing, flirting—whose youth will have been stolen, confiscated by the monster of the theocratic state.

THE NEW CITIZEN

From Repression to Violence

One of the greatest disappointments of the decolonized individual was his belief in an end to violence. In fact it is everywhere, explosive or latent, military or institutional, and it expresses itself inside and outside the country, even with close allies. After decades of independence they are still cutting throats in Algeria, imprisoning people in Tunisia, torturing in Cuba, and condemning the uncovered faces of women in Iran and Algeria. Mass graves have been discovered in Iraq; populations fleeing before imminent massacre have been counted in the hundreds of thousands, abandoning their dead and often the young along the way.

In addition to economic exploitation and cultural alienation, colonization is the history of a succession of unbearable constraints. It has typically been characterized by periodic outbursts, which are met with by savage repression, followed by a resigned calm, until the next crisis arises. Yet, even with liberation, the violence continued, the faces were just about the same, the executioners the same. There are not that many ways to torture, to deprive someone of his freedom or his life. Some commentators will say that this was necessary to consolidate the country's growing power against potential enemies, sometimes even against militants in the independence movement, men and women who had until then been completely devoted but who failed to understand that the revolution was over and it was absurd — dangerous, in fact — to assume that every promise would be kept. We know that social upheavals afford an opportunity to settle old scores and are no less horrifying than the various struggles for liberation. Bourguiba, the founder of modern Tunisia, liquidated the rivals who had tried to assassinate him. Algeria executed a large number of its early leaders and still has not emerged from its

49

THE NEW CITIZEN

deadly struggles. Morocco owes its relative calm to the iron-fisted rule of the monarchy and its servants, which did little or nothing to prevent several attempts on the sovereign's life. Perhaps an enlightened despotism is needed when countries are still young. Ben-Gurion, the labor leader and first prime minister of Israel, did not hesitate to shell a ship filled with weapons that had been leased by his adversaries, who were themselves nationalist Jews, after he had negotiated a truce with the English occupying force. Then there are the inevitable missteps and errors, the corruption of the new government. Bourguiba, initially idolized by the nation, faced food riots and political agitation, all of which he attributed to his minister of the interior—whom he fired. Then, as the difficulties increased, the restrictions of an increasingly threatened government led him to hang his fundamentalist opponents to ensure his survival. In the liberated ex-third world, imprisonment and execution have probably been used more frequently since independence than under the colonial regimes.

Naturally, there are degrees of violence, ranging from simple police intimidation to military intervention. Dissuasion ranges from the continuous presence of police in an ever-tightening net from which no one escapes, to assassination and imprisonment, judicial and extrajudicial. Delinquency, even minor, and unauthorized opinions are brutally and immediately repressed, such repression often extending to entire families. If there is recidivism, the accused, now considered beyond redemption, disappears without a word. But first he will be tortured to determine the importance of the crime. His death will depend not on the application of the law but on the mood of the ruler, on the degree of cynicism found among those in power. In general, the government can claim success: submission is apparently interiorized, with the populace's behavior and thinking being aligned with government demands.

50

THE NEW CITIZEN

But from time to time the decolonized will lead two lives. The first, the public life, reveals a citizen respectful of order, an admirer of the national leader, a sincere and faithful, even satisfied, believer. The second is private; here the citizen ignores religious obligations and discreetly violates the prescriptions of the Koran. He will make do with the obvious emoluments. Aside from personal enrichment and the benefits it brings, there will be the ostentatious display of wealth common to every new middle class: opulent secondary residences in doubtful taste, preferably not too far from the presidential palace, a powerful late-model car, a profusion of canvases by local painters, noisy parties that keep the entire neighborhood awake at night to display his generosity. After all, schizophrenia is also a way of life.

For those who, in spite of everything, upset the status quo and appear to question, if not threaten, the system, force is always available. In Black Africa there has never been a period of generalized calm, entire ethnic groups are massacred. The Ivory Coast, once the most beautiful showcase in Africa, has fallen back into chaos. Congo-Kinshasa has never known peace. In Algeria the army has maintained a reign of terror for years without managing to eradicate its adversaries. In southern Tunisia there have been discreet battles between dissidents and the small national army.

Violence is not limited to the national scene. It infects relations among the young nations, sapping national vitality. But they act as if no other solution was available. Take the irksome problem of borders, for example. These were created by the colonizers to divide the spoils, especially at the famous Treaty of Berlin. They have remained as a kind of poison legacy. Why have those nations not tried, through negotiation or some lasting agreement, to work toward the transformation of an absurd topographical configuration? Instead, Morocco

THE NEW CITIZEN

and Algeria have gone to war and maintained a low-level conflict through the Polisario Front. Libya has invaded Chad and been punished by an Egyptian expedition under the pretext of terminating a fratricidal war, which resulted in fifty thousand deaths. Syria militarily occupies Lebanon, which it treats as a kind of maritime province. North and South Korea have continued to exhaust one another in an interminable confrontation and both sides maintain standing armies. War is endemic to Black Africa, and international or interethnic conflicts have created more victims than colonization. Such terrible losses have not been seen since the worst periods of slavery. However, those losses were unintentional. Although it is true that only one in four slaves survived the voyage in the hold of the ship that brought them to the plantations of the New World, slave traders had no desire to see their cargo destroyed. Unfortunately, the current warfare among the black populations of Africa is not concerned with profitability; its horrors have greatly exceeded those of the raids once conducted jointly by prominent blacks and Arab traders to supply the European slave trade. The colonists, except for occasional massacres when they felt threatened, had no interest in destroying their labor force. This, rather than morality and compassion, is what established the limits of colonization.

Why such continued desperate violence? The embarrassed historians among the formerly colonized have not failed to look for explanations. They claim this is simply a bad habit inherited from the colonial period, an additional wound. They note that there was considerably less of an emotional outpouring when the colonized suffered at the hands of the colonizers. So be it. We try to relieve our sense of guilt any way we can. But now the violence occurs among the formerly colonized, against their own people. In spite of the passage of

THE NEW CITIZEN

time, the situation has not only endured, it has gotten worse. The upheavals during the wars of independence are not so far in the past, but then, as we are reminded, it was a matter of terrorizing an adversary. Who is being terrorized now? Anyone who has visited South Africa has heard talk of the use of "necklaces" of burning tires to destroy political opponents or even economic rivals. Television has broadcast pictures of the suffering of the victims of interethnic massacres, imploring their executioners not to save their life but to shoot them—the gun being a far more expedient and less terrifying weapon than the machete. In Algeria children have had their throats cut in front of their parents' eyes, and parents have been executed in front of their children. During decolonization, French soldiers had their penises cut off and stuffed in their mouths. Hatred, it is said, bred such kinds of perversion. Should such abominable practices be continued? Is it necessary to cut the nose off someone who smokes during Ramadan? Or to stuff pipe bombs with nails in order to increase the suffering of the survivors? Should we tolerate kidnappings, a specialty in Bolivia, or the abduction of children born to mixed marriages in the Maghreb?

There is violence in every society. Perhaps, more fundamentally, we have not yet been able to control the violence within us. We have only managed to confront it with some other violence, rather than banning all forms of violence. The Christians, in spite of the teachings of their founder, have been at war continuously, even among themselves, sometimes under the banner of their spiritual leaders. They have not been so quick to abandon the destruction of heretics, more important than the destruction of infidels: massacres, burnings, and torture are commonplace occurrences in their shared history. But eventually they abandoned such practices.

53

THE NEW CITIZEN

This obstinacy in the use of violence may be the proof of our inadequate degree of socialization, of our animal nature. However, human progress is also an attempt to ritualize violence to protect society's members from mutual destruction. At present the world's formerly colonized societies, regardless of the form of government, can hardly be said to have succeeded in this. Is it possible they contain more latent violence than other societies, which is reflected in their destructive and self-destructive behavior? Why did the pillagers of Baghdad, after emptying the residences of their former leaders, need also to destroy and sometimes burn them? It is as if pillage and arson cannot be explained by poverty but by a kind of pure, almost disinterested violence. Thus the French revolutionaries of 1789 burned the splendid palaces of the royal family and the nobles, along with ecclesiastical buildings, rather than preserving them as part of a shared heritage. Violence—and war, which is its generalized expression—is the sign of an eclipse of the nascent rule of law, that is, a perpetuation of the jungle.

A Nation Born Too Late

For a nation to exist it must have a common vision to enable it to develop internally and, externally, win its place among other nations, against them if need be. But there is no point in having a plan unless it is felt to be, in some measure, realizable. Yet within many young nations tyranny blocks all progress, focuses the nation's energies on the tyrant and his cronies. The decolonized nations are like the children of aging parents, born weak and suffering, the fruit having dried before it has had a chance to mature. The national project of the decolonized seems to be exhausted before it has really begun, primarily because those nations suffer from a

THE NEW CITIZEN

historical handicap—they have been born too late. There are many reasons for this: the apathy caused by colonization, which continues long after independence, the persistent lethargy of the people, the vagueness of the concept of national territory, which has only been recently established, the continued enticements of a supranational body of nations. We easily forget that Western colonization took over from the Turks, who maintained the Arabs as their vassals for centuries. This misfortune has not been entirely overcome and may no longer be surmountable.

Following the initial excitement associated with the rediscovery of a national identity, some of the decolonized joked (humor is never completely innocent, however) about regretting the colonial period. Naturally, those were dangerous times, but the struggle was more uplifting than the current stasis. One aspired to freedom, to take advantage of victory. What good is all that now when there is no one or no thing to fight against, nothing to struggle for? The old weariness seems to rise to the surface.

There is yet another paradox to the decolonized's national aspiration: his nation has come into existence at a time when the Western national ideal that served as a model has begun to weaken throughout the rest of the world. It is no longer the bright new engine that led the majority of Europe into the nineteenth century. Perhaps we are witnessing the end of nation-states. The new Europe, which is forming for better or worse, has been created largely in opposition to the traditional nations, which, their historical missions accomplished, appear to be ready to exit the historical stage. Soon they will come to resemble an empire, much like the United States, or even India or China, which, contrary to appearances, have never been nations in the European sense.

The decolonized is thus led to engage in a zigzag march

55

between an increasingly frayed national present and a distant utopian future. Having had his fill of the pleasures of independence, he is barely moved by the signs and symbols of sovereignty: flags, the burgeoning number of diplomatic bodies, increasingly strident displays of cultural identity, receptions with well-stocked buffets. But not everyone has access to such benefits and you can't live on cocktails alone. The decolonized will need visas to travel, which he will have to bargain for since he is not a national of a major power, and dollars, which will be issued parsimoniously, because his currency is too weak on the international markets and not convertible, making it little better than worthless. He is forced to acknowledge that his nation is too fragile to avoid being, in one way or another, a satellite, and that independence, obtained with such difficulty, remains threatened.

Should we again return to that illustrious "Arab nation," the hope of utopians who continue to dream of a grandiose past, a nation that was never really a nation, much like the Ottoman Empire, even though Islam unified half the known world? But history marches on, the decolonized knows this. Could Iranians, Syrians, and Maghrebians all be consolidated into a single group? In North Africa alone similar conceptions of custom and freedom are not universally shared. Tunisia and Libya have tried to merge, an effort that lasted no longer than the time it took their respective leaders to change their mind. The same is true of Egypt and Syria. Europe and the United States, which are envied and admired in spite of the resentment, have access to a continuous territorial space. Given the diversity of interests involved, how could an Arab-Muslim empire stretching from the Atlantic Ocean to India be created anew, without destroying it in the process? At present, Morocco, Algeria, and Tunisia are more interested in forming

THE NEW CITIZEN

alliances with other nearby Mediterranean nations, Italy or France, for example, nations with which they now share a certain demographic community, than with the Muslim populations of Pakistan or Indonesia.

Naturally, there is the glue of religion, proposed or imposed by fundamentalists, probably as much by calculation as by conviction. Aside from the exaggerated attention given to sporadic movements, we tend to ignore the equally important awakening of the indifferent, the hesitant, and the incredulous. We focus on a handful of young firebrands, who abandon jeans for djellabas, pretending to ignore the majority. Nowhere does there exist, as many claim to believe, a true religious renewal; believers and nonbelievers alike remain pretty much as they were. On the other hand, there have been attempts to use religion for political ends with the intent of winning a larger role in the concert of nations through a strategy of fundamentalism. But those who are incredulous, let's say the discreet agnostic, can no longer pretend to have faith when their religious practice is based on conformity and solidarity. What would happen if the fundamentalists were to succeed? Should the decolonized subject abandon all the things he has acquired—admittedly often borrowed from the West—which have now become customary and a part of his personality? In more general terms, he knows that the resources of the irrational and shared emotions are no longer sufficient for meeting the challenges of the modern world he hopes to become a part of. It is unlikely he will find in the Koran the secrets of industrialization or ways to refertilize the African steppe.

The decolonized experiences a form of stationary dismemberment, torn and pulled from every side. In such cases the nation-state exhausts itself before it has had an opportunity

THE NEW CITIZEN

to fully affirm itself, because it is unable to develop the new society demanded by the younger generations, taught by television to look beyond their borders and hungry for new experiences. Day-to-day existence is organized to a degree but punctuated by corruption and repression. Even the boldest of governments, after a few timid efforts at reform, subsides into the general paralysis. Innovation engenders fear, which leads to resistance and public disturbances. When the Tunisian Ben Ali, who succeeded Bourguiba, tried to preserve the gains made by his predecessor, Saudi Arabia intervened, forcing him to reverse course on women's rights and hasten the Islamization of the country.

Does the decolonized then dream, or boast, of the two golden ages of Arab unification: that of North Africa and the caliphate of Baghdad—more a feature of the *Thousand and One Nights* than of historical reality—when the Arabs were opulent, generous, and open to the fecundity of science, art, and philosophy? He knows that this is, more than anything, the substance of a now outdated myth. Of what value today are the sciences of the period, such as the medicine of the Middle Ages, that he continues to take pride in? It is no more than a curiosity of history, something to be consigned to the museum of progress. In Black Africa, where a supernation never existed, everything would have to be invented, and there have been efforts to that effect. Moreover, there is the question of whether such myths are harmful, at least when they are first promulgated, for in order to bring them to fruition, the current order must be overturned. In any event, a return to fundamentalism would be the negation of the Arab-Muslim nations, whose governments know it would mean their destruction. The fundamentalists know it too. For with the end of the national ideal, they will have eliminated the handful of freedoms those nations managed to provide in

58

spite of everything: the relaxation of religious control and the control over private life, the alleviation of female servitude, the adoption of laws shared by other nations.

Nations without Law

The absence of law is worse than an unjust law. An unjust law is a reparable disorder; the absence of law implies the rule of an arbitrary system, where anything can happen to anyone. Foreigners grow indignant that there are few criticisms of ongoing corruption, the control by those close to the leader of various economic sectors, and the questionable enrichment of certain individuals. People are scandalized that there are so few inquiries concerning the abuse of power, such as the abduction of a political rival, a journalist, or simply a critic, whose family will never know if he is dead or alive. Such attitudes are extremely naive. Tyranny is opaque by its very nature. It could not operate in daylight. It would need to justify its decisions, supply proofs — things that define a democracy. But democracy remains foreign to the political practices of the third world, especially the Arab-Muslim world.

Even during the period of colonization, when the law was on the side of the colonizer, there were limits to illegality. The colonizer was forced, although unwillingly, to consider the citizens back home. They, not being overly concerned with the interests of the colonists, were sufficiently democratic to impose a common set of laws throughout the empire. Once colonial law was abolished, it was never really replaced. The ruler owes nothing to anyone. He prevents the development of intermediary powers with sufficient autonomy — a judicial system, for example — that could serve as buffers between himself and the decolonized, who, in the event of litigation, are forced to turn directly to him, the only effective judge.

THE NEW CITIZEN

The consequence of this unlimited power is the possibility of limitless iniquity. In this sense, there is no difference between the states of the Maghreb and the worst tyrannical regimes of Black Africa. Behind a more civilized appearance, the previous sultan of Morocco established a series of prisons that were far worse than those of the colonizer, and for decades hounded the wives and children of the condemned.

The absence of law is not new, of course. Colonized peoples have always been subject to the will of those in power, often dependent on a yet more powerful entity, directly authorized by God. The bey of Tunis or the dey of Algiers had the right of life and death over their subjects, but they themselves were subject to the Ottoman court, for whom they were theoretically only representatives. No one's life was safe. The Wahabite regime of Saudi Arabia, so typical of the orthodox Muslim world, simply perpetuates an earlier tradition. It was hoped that a revolt against the colonizer would help overturn such feudal customs. The revolution never took place. After a grace period, at the end of his life, Bourguiba, a socializing and democratic leader, the father of his people's independence, transformed himself into an autocrat, worse than the old sovereign whom he had pointlessly mistreated and ruined. The presidents of the new republics generally mimic what is most arbitrary about the colonial power.

The ruler's relative freedom of action, which is unimpeded, multiplies the temptation to provide preferential treatment, resulting in random condemnations that are not proportional to the crime, contrary to what is found in any rational jurisdiction. A passing remark made in a café can lead to prison, a suspicion can destroy a career. France, with sixty million inhabitants, has fifty thousand people in prison; the small island of Cuba has 150,000, in most cases for nothing more than their opinions; the majority of them have been jailed without

THE NEW CITIZEN

trial or after a perfunctory trial by a cowed court. Naturally, this gives the police a nebulous but unlimited power, because they have the ruler's confidence. A Cuban joke has it that Havana has a million police for two million citizens. And the immobility of the regime allows no room to hope for any immediate change. What is needed is its total collapse. Yet every disturbance results in increased repression. In 1981 a state of emergency was declared in Egypt; it has never been abolished. The only demonstrations that are permitted are those that provide some form of diversion: displays of support for Afghanistan (although the Taliban are feared), Palestine (of course), or Iraq (even if there is some hesitation because of its excesses). These are so many escape valves, authoritarian vents, which help convince the populace that it possesses a semblance of freedom. The country of the decolonized is a country without law, where there is rampant institutional violence that can only be countered by even greater violence. The fundamentalists know this and await their moment. The "law of God" they hope to establish, the law of the priests, will suppress even the few scraps of freedom that have been conceded by the ruler. It will void the law for the sake of religious dogma.

A Sick Society

Here I wish to address what has been called Islamic terrorism. The world finds itself faced with a situation that has left it exasperated and lacking any coherent explanation. Terrorism is not only morally scandalous but senseless, irrational. Yet even the irrational has its own logic, and immorality its defense: Islamic terrorism is an extreme form of the continuous violence that wracks the Arab world. It is not even an unusual phenomenon, and "God's madmen" of the Muslim

THE NEW CITIZEN

religion are no crazier than any others. In Vietnam local food stalls were used to hide bombs that killed without distinction: Americans, French, Vietnamese. Algerian nationalists used Vietnam as a model. Even public suicide is not new. Korean bonzes set themselves ablaze to impress the Europeans. Readers may recall the name Palach, the Czech student who set himself on fire in a public square to influence the direction of politics in his country. The common ground in all these cases is a self-sacrificial act, a technique most civilizations are not eager to employ. Even the Muslim kamikaze believes in a better life than the one on Earth, in a paradisal afterlife that will serve as recompense for his devotion. Yet even this characteristic is not original. Isn't this what all believers cling to, both members of the clergy and the lay public, who are looking for confirmation by history? Although we are right to denounce the immorality of blind acts of violence that strike indiscriminately, do the pilots who bomb a city worry about who their victims are? Is this the first time that political or patriotic considerations have won out over moral principles? For extremists, how important is the harm caused to bystanders compared to what they judge to be the importance of their cause? For terrorist leaders, political murder is not assassination but an episode in an ongoing war. To understand terrorism, even in its suicidal form, we must not only consider it from the point of view of its victims, who are necessarily and quite legitimately angered by their suffering, but from the perspective of its leaders and followers. Not only does its meaning differ for the two camps, but it fails to arouse the same sense of indignation: "It's our way of fighting," explains a Palestinian leader, "since we don't have planes or tanks."

It's not that novelty has made suicide bombing original, but that its radicality and generality have turned it into an original form of warfare. The bonzes killed only themselves.

THE NEW CITIZEN

Without exception, the pilot who drops his bombs on a target hopes they avoid the innocent. The Muslim kamikaze wants to kill not only himself but the greatest number of people possible, guilty and innocent, combatants and noncombatants alike. These two deaths are linked: since he does not care about his own life, he need not concern himself with that of the others. "A true Muslim would be able to sacrifice his parents and children," stated Mulana Sayed Abdullah Bukhari, imam of the largest mosque in New Delhi. The Iranians had no qualms about exposing children to clouds of Iraqi poison gas, each of them with a key to paradise hanging from his neck. If they were willing to sacrifice their own children, why would they worry about someone else's? The kamikaze's actions incorporate the idea that he will never return; he knows, and accepts, that he will not survive. Every society produces its own heroes, who offer their life for the survival of the group. But heroes do not renounce life, they risk it, which is why they merit praise, even when they aspire to glory. The doctor or missionary who travels to a country in which there is an epidemic knows that he might fall victim to the disease, and possibly die, but he does not seek death. We know today that, contrary to what Japanese propaganda claimed, the Japanese kamikaze pilots were not so light-hearted about their imminent death. The Arab kamikaze expects nothing other than death, and he awaits it willingly. It is in this sense that he is unique. For in this case the certainty of death abolishes everything, makes everything here on Earth negligible, insignificant, including any legal sanctions. The suicide bomber denies the rules so painfully acquired by human societies, the outline of a moralization of war. It is a reversal of the gradual humanization of human societies. They cut the throats of journalists, who are only doing their job, abduct or machine-gun tourists, who have arrived from

THE NEW CITIZEN

another part of the world and had the misfortune to want to amuse themselves. A tract that appeared in Casablanca before a horrendous attack, one that was distributed only in the mosques, exhorted its readers to make no exceptions for women or children—all of them were considered guilty and deserved to die. The same justification has been advanced by Palestinian leaders: all Israelis without exception must be attacked. Islamic terrorism appears to have declared war on the entire world, including the Arab countries that fail to align themselves with its objectives. Tunisia, Morocco, even Saudi Arabia, the leading sanctuary of the Arab-Muslim world, have been struck. Until recently, Palestinian bombers concentrated on Israeli or Jewish targets; now the battle has extended to the world at large.

Yet such aberrations are far from being universally denounced in the Arab world. Not all Arabs have become "God's madmen" but we often encounter a sense of embarrassed indulgence or uneasiness rather than any firm condemnation, and occasionally even a kind of grateful—and not very subtle – admiration. "We are all bin Laden!" was a cry frequently heard in the suburbs of Paris, the streets of Cairo, and Ramallah immediately after September 11, 2001. There was a sense of pride and the satisfaction of revenge; as if those young idlers had contributed to the destruction of the New York skyscrapers. Bin Laden is considered the collective arm of the entire Arab-Muslim community. The hijackers, the advanced technological version of the makers of homemade bombs, sacrificed themselves for all Islam. They were considered "martyrs." The kamikaze is not an isolated individual, a "madman" who acts under the influence of some uncontrolled impulse. He is recruited and trained in camps, supported by technical teams, given a Saudi or Pakistani passport, more recently English or French, and financed by the Arab governments. This diversity, which spans geographic regions, feeds a confused but reassuring sense of solidarity, the exalted feeling of a rediscovered sense of popular power. The painful cry of powerlessness, "They're killing Muslims," is answered by the suicide bomber who acts in the name of all Muslims.

But such rhetoric, even when translated into bloodthirsty acts, is an admission of weakness. "We don't have any planes, and the Arab governments who do don't dare use them. They're traitors." Which implies: "We have no choice. We must resign ourselves to such individual actions. We are borne along by a history beyond our control."

To employ the language of medicine, we could say that Arab-Muslim society suffers from a serious depressive syndrome that prevents it from seeing any way out of its current situation. The Arab world has still not found, or has not wanted to consider, the transformations that would enable it to adapt to the modern world, which it cannot help but absorb. Rather than examining itself and applying the proper remedies, it looks for the causes of its disability in others. It's the fault of the Americans, or the Jews, of unbelievers, infidels, or multinationals. Without underestimating the role of its relations with its global partners, or the rise to power of the American empire, which took over where the colonizers left off, it would be more useful to inquire into the internal causes of this stagnation. Through a classic process of projection, the Arab world blames them for every sin, depravity, loss of value, materialism, atheism, and so on. The suicide bomber must destroy this abject world along with himself, for it has become unlivable for him and those like him. It is the job of his handlers to convince him. It's not just a question of poverty, as some would have it, but the confrontation of two societies, one open, adventurous, dynamic, and therefore filled

THE NEW CITIZEN

with danger, wicked and depraved, the other, static, turned inward, powerless to confront this challenge but virtuous and legitimate through its submission to God. Incapable of acting, Arab society finds relief only in crisis, murderous outbursts of anger against those presumed to be guilty. Islamic terrorism is only one of the most alarming symptoms of this powerlessness. The others, less threatening, are no less significant. The absence of democracy, corruption, the fragility and unfairness of the judicial system, the condition of women—isolation, the violence of clitoral excision, the lack of legal rights, which has a direct impact on the education of the children in their care, who perpetuate such ignorance—sexual bullying, the delayed circumcision that risks causing long-lasting trauma, the frustration arising from separation of the sexes, the power of religion, which interferes with the proper operation of an unfettered rationality, the persecution of intellectuals, and the destruction of critical spirit, all form a coherent negative ensemble.

All of this would be exacerbated if the terrorist actions of the Arab world were effective. But through its attacks, including in recalcitrant or hesitant Arab countries, terrorism has triggered total war without possessing the means to win it. It risks provoking a global response. Although Europe hesitates, the United States understood and, even before September 11, 2001, was making preparations. Scorning shared laws, Islamic terrorism has operated outside the law, which has produced a highly damaging representation of Arab-Muslim society. So that, rather than relieving its suffering, it maintains it within a vicious circle: uncontrolled violence arouses worldwide hostility, and this hostility increases suffering.

THE NEW CITIZEN

Going Abroad

In this listless environment, interspersed with convulsive nightmares, from time to time there arises a sense of remorse: the rulers of various decolonized states gather with great pomp in one of their capitals, sometimes in national costume to add a sense of drama to their meeting. There are embraces, compliments are exchanged and promises made. Sometimes warnings are issued, invectives; solemn declarations are written in which traitors are stigmatized and accusations are leveled at the world as a whole. Then each participant, flanked by his bodyguards, is swallowed by his Mercedes and returns home to ordinary life, as if nothing had happened.

A few of the more courageous journalists, a handful of fractious intellectuals, mostly living abroad, once again ask, with anger or melancholy, why no serious project has ever come out of these prestigious gatherings. They forget, or pretend to forget, that the rulers are immobile by nature and by desire. They have no sincere project to offer since they are incapable of offering one, and moreover do not wish to.

The fact is that the decolonized quickly discovers they are faced with a lack of perspective. Once more they are forced to make a painful assessment: if decolonization leads to expectations that are economic, political, and cultural, they must resign themselves to accepting the fact that their country has not fully succeeded in any of the three areas. It does not enjoy widespread prosperity comparable to that of the Western nations, or democracy, the face and guarantee of liberty, or an expansion of the arts, literature, and knowledge, the products of critical investigation. But most of all there is no foreseeable hope of change, just an endless stream of lost illusions. "Maybe we're not ready for democracy," a colleague confided to me with a sigh. When I tried to reassure him by object-

67

THE NEW CITIZEN

ing that there had been a number of interesting attempts in Black Africa, he responded maliciously, "Yes, but look where it's gotten them. Chaos! We may be catatonic, but they, they are in deep shit."

Is there a choice between tyranny and permanent disorder? What can be done in the face of an apparently incurable illness, other than to resign oneself to it or flee? Faced with a dead-end future, the decolonized dream of escape. They are, in effect, potential émigrés, virtual immigrants within their own country, which seems to them increasingly limited and oppressive.

Should they decide to leave, why not consider the country of the colonizer? They will set aside their former problems, now somewhat softened by time, and concentrate on the best moments of colonization—the beaches and summer nights, friendships. They are already elsewhere, as if the dream could one day become reality. They travel, first as tourists or for health reasons, visit relatives. If they have additional means, they will invest them there and follow fortune, without repatriating the profits. If they still have doubts, they can claim that they are not going to rejoin the former colonizer but "the Frenchman of France," which in the past was a quality label, a sign of freedom, respect for the law, possibly of equality. Isn't that the motto of the French Republic: *Liberté, Égalité, Fraternité?* They are already familiar with the culture. They speak the language, which will considerably facilitate life for an immigrant. Don't they already willingly buy their products? When they visit their relatives or friends, those who have already made the move and settled in Paris, Lyons, or Marseilles, they have the impression of returning to a familiar land. For that matter, the country has been described as an earthly paradise. They are encouraged to join their former countrymen to avoid being alone,

68

THE NEW CITIZEN

to enlarge the community, like tourists who, to convince themselves they've made the right choice, recall the wonders and marvels of their vacation, whatever the reality may have been. After all, when their own cousins returned from abroad they were driving new cars filled with gadgets, washing machines, radios, televisions, all of which were sold on the spot, including the car. Entire families live off the money sent back home by a husband, son, or brother.

Just in case, they will begin to gather information, concretely this time, about the labor market. If they possess any technical skills, they hope it will be easier to find a job. For the blue-collar worker it will still be easier to swell the ranks of day laborers, sidewalk sweepers, or street cleaners, one of those jobs it would seem that the spoiled youth of the rich countries no longer desire. If there are further doubts, a residue of guilt about leaving home, they will persuade themselves that they really have no choice. Intellectuals must balance between exile and silence, that is, spiritual death, the mask or flight. Surely, there will be more intellectuals and writers abroad, preferably in the former colonizing country, than in their homeland. And paradoxically, they will express themselves more freely, for in those host countries, which they continue to denounce out of habit and through solidarity with their people, they are allowed to speak freely without risk. Paradoxically, this also works in favor of fundamentalists, who can vehemently proclaim their faith and their demands because they enjoy a freedom of expression they would not tolerate back home if they held power. The imams of London are more openly vehement than those of Saudi Arabia. A French Muslim, implicated in the attacks, calmly stated, "France will become an Islamic state, without question." Curiously, the danger will continue to come from their home country, which will never forgive their departure

THE NEW CITIZEN

and their timid remarks: for they take it upon themselves, and from abroad no less, to criticize their own people! This will be the decade of Salman Rushdie and Taslima Nasreen. They will be denounced and physically threatened, although by going into exile they will do a better job of serving truth and their own people than if they had remained at home.

Naturally, all those potential dreamers will never leave. They are too old for adventure, could never begin a new life; they are tied by their connections and attachments, their assets. But the youngest, the most vigorous, those who have nothing to lose, will one day try to make the dream a reality. Young "hittites" talk only about the letters they receive from those who have left, now living in places where work is not a rare commodity; where it is said the women in the street are free to do as they please; where you can express yourself out loud, even in public, even against the leaders, without being arrested and thrown into prison; where you're protected by the law and the courts; where there are economic advantages; where you receive help, even if it is from a foreigner; where medical care is free; where everything is possible, while back home almost nothing is. During the first visit of the president of the French Republic since decolonization, did young Algerians shout like young people everywhere, "Down with X! Long live Y!" while fighting the police protecting the illustrious visitor? No. To the shame of their country's officials, they shouted "Visas! Visas!" They indicated they were intent on leaving their country, preferably with all their papers in order. But we know the lack of papers will not stop them; and they will risk their life if need be, crossing the sea, crossing borders. Isn't paradise worth the risk? What else is there to dream about in purgatory except paradise?

The Immigrant

The Blessings of Exile

Although I have been developing the idea for some time, it is fortunate in a way that I did not undertake this portrait of the decolonized subject earlier. Two significant characteristics would have been missing: the growth of immigration and the considerable increase in violence. These are not neutral phenomena, they are significant of both the true condition of formerly colonized nations and their current relations with the rest of the world.

Immigration is not specific to decolonization; it has existed in the majority of economically or politically backward countries for years. It is the product of poverty and fear, hunger and frustration, an apparently hopeless future. History is also the history of migrations and, therefore, of intermarriage. Ancient Greece and the entire Mediterranean basin were the theater of incessant population movements. Italy, Ireland especially, Portugal, and Spain have participated in these massive waves of immigration. It is possible that we have entered an era of global disruption, when the movement of populations will begin to accelerate. It has assumed a specific physiognomy in the formerly colonized nations, for it results from a more or less manifest conjunction of individual desire, the complaisance of governments, and the hesitation of the host countries.

Under the influence of religion, which favors unrestricted

reproduction, and irresponsible policies that are often deliberately centered on increased birthrates, the resulting unlimited growth has produced a large population of turbulent and often delinquent youth—mostly because of underemployment—that sees no option other than emigration. But in spite of growing resources, these governments are less and less capable of handling the increased demand for them, or providing even the minimum requirements, and the temptation has been great to encourage population decline. Although they did nothing to openly promote immigration, they did nothing to oppose it, sometimes even lending a helping hand. Morocco has dissuaded its immigrants from returning home. The Democratic Republic of Congo has made determined efforts to keep theirs in Europe for good. Contrary to their diplomatic statements, far from considering smugglers as criminals, traffickers of human flesh who, according to Europeans, abuse their unfortunate victims, these governments provide them with administrative facilities, protected gathering places where people can wait until their departure for the French or Italian coast, a temporary stop before their ultimate arrival in Germany or Great Britain. The presence of women and children, who pay only half price, is favored because their presence is said to diminish the zeal of customs agents.

Aside from the relief provided by these demographic purges, the rulers of third-world countries have discovered other, indirect, benefits from this growing pressure on European nations. They can discreetly negotiate a slowdown of these unstoppable human waves against certain benefits: access to fishing zones, more beneficial loans or exchanges, reduction of customs tariffs, and so on. A leader of a black country was quite frank about this. "No one in Europe could stop immigration," he said, which is probably accurate. We

THE IMMIGRANT

can do little against the survival impulse. He made the error of adding, cynically, "If necessary, we will build bridges between Africa and Europe!" Another, somewhat less diplomatic, warned, "From now on Africa is going to cling to your backside!" These are so many avowals of a policy favorable to immigration. The capricious and imprudent Libyan Colonel Khadafi, who for years financed terrorist movements throughout the world, and who had to renounce open violence following a punitive American raid, turned to immigration as a new and less compromising weapon in pursuing his war against the West. Turks, Nigerians, Somalis, and Moroccans assemble in Libya before being piled into small boats, where the unlucky voyagers must, for lack of space, sometimes remain standing for the entire crossing. Even the prudent Tunisians are not strangers to such trafficking and willingly allow use of their ports, which are well known to the local population. Unfortunately, the greed of the smugglers, overloaded boats, deplorable sanitary conditions, and the subterfuges required to maintain clandestinity sometimes result in misfortune. But none of this has dampened the desire of the immigrants. We can at least hope that the sleep of their rulers has not been disturbed.

It is as if immigration, far from being considered harmful or embarrassing, has become, for many third-world countries, both a necessity and a bargaining chip. For some it may be an element of the competition that inevitably occurs among nations, especially between the powerful and prosperous and the weak and impoverished. More generally, from the perspective of global geopolitics, immigration could even be a tool of peaceful expansion. Migratory Islamization has been spoken of in just such terms.

Naturally, the immigrant is, as an individual, foreign to these considerations. If he resolves the insoluble problem

THE IMMIGRANT

of a visa, if he survives the dangerous voyage, incredibly precarious in an age when an airplane ticket can take you halfway around the world, if he doesn't drown or suffocate or freeze in the back of a truck, if he manages, led by rapacious but effective guides, to overcome the vigilance of customs agents, if he is not unmasked at the last moment and turned back, having finally overcome all the obstacles in this game of chance, which uses men as pawns, he will come to believe he has finally escaped his purgatory. He would gladly throw himself facedown on the ground and kiss the soil of what he believes to be a new Eldorado.

Failure Twice Over

The Maghrebi immigrant is, in this sense, privileged. In addition to the endorsement of his own government, he benefits from the relative tolerance of the host country's consulate, where he obtains a tourist visa, which he intends to extend—with or without the approval of the authorities—at the risk of going underground. If he has the money, he will land at Orly airport, if not, at Marseilles. After a quiet crossing he will travel from the Gare Saint-Charles to the Gare de Lyon in Paris. The trip often brings back memories, since he has already spent his vacations in France. This time, though, it's serious, it's for good. But he's not too worried. After all, isn't he familiar with the culture and even the customs of the former colonial government? He arrives at these conclusions without the doubts and reservations common to colonial subjects.

Where will he go? Taxis that specialize in their own form of highway robbery are waiting for him. The price they charge is well above the legally approved rate and is arbitrarily chosen for arriving immigrants, regardless of their origin or destination. He is not traveling to the fashionable quarters of Paris,

THE IMMIGRANT

of course. If he were, he would have already rented, through an agency or through friends, a lovely apartment or even a house with a garden on the Champ-de-Mars or in one of the wealthy suburbs of the city. But in that case he would no longer be an immigrant but a "friend of France," who has come to spend freely among the busy stores in those well-to-do neighborhoods. The real immigrant will be driven to the home of a brother, a cousin, a friend, the friend of a friend, in one of the projects situated on the outskirts of Paris or Lyons that have replaced the slums of earlier generations. Here rents are cheaper and it's easy to find a friendly café, a place to worship, and familiar foods—grains, spices, meat.

But here he will learn that the Eldorado described by his friends, the promised land so ardently desired, is no longer what it was. It's harder to find a job, and the police keep a watchful eye. He will enter into a vicious circle of his own. To obtain work he'll need a residence card; to obtain a residence card, he'll need to have a job. On the street, in the subway, it seems—possibly it's just his imagination—that people don't look at him in quite the same way as they did back home. At best they speak to him with a suspicious politeness or forced friendliness. Nothing is quite as natural as he would have liked and he hardly feels welcome. Like most exiles, he harbors an uneasy sense of recognition for his adopted country, which requires no more than that he make a show of his newfound loyalty. He finds, with some bitterness, that this love, which he was so ready to give, is not appreciated by his fellow citizens. He discovers that immigration, far from being the solution to his problems, fails on two fronts: that of his home country and that of the host country.

Obviously, he knows about the situation back home, that's why he left. Immigration is one of the additional signs of the inability of young nations to resolve their internal problems,

THE IMMIGRANT

primarily to feed their population and provide them with a minimum of comfort and freedom. Without this minimum sense of well-being, growth, in every sense of the word, is impossible and the temptation to revolt exacerbated. But if, by accepting immigration, by encouraging it, one gains a certain peace of mind, this is accompanied by a loss of substance, the loss of a large number of healthy young men, often the most enterprising and the most gifted, not only manual workers but technicians, executives, and intellectuals, who are seduced by the hope of a more lucrative and more agreeable life abroad. A large number of medical students, trained in European universities, fail to return home once their studies are completed, even though their homeland desperately needs medical practitioners. In the Caribbean it is said that the end of slavery brought with it the freedom to expatriate.

Except for a handful of avant-garde intellects, for the former colonist the immigrant serves as a living reminder of the country's colonial enterprise, a time when the French flag flew over immense swaths of land and France ruled over a numerous and diverse people. Even though he lacked enthusiasm for these exploits, the presence of the immigrant is the residue of a collective mourning, a separation born of violence, where his was the losing side. Now that the divorce is final, what does his former partner want? He has what he wanted: a state, a government, even an army. Why does he want to settle in the nation he claims to despise? Even if the French national could erase the past, even if his conscience was completely clear, the presence of the immigrant prevents him from forgetting what was a glorious past for some, scandalous for others. The Maghrebian is not a Russian or Romanian immigrant, a foreigner who has arrived here by accident; he is the bastard of the colonial adventure, a living reproach or permanent disappointment. The French national

THE IMMIGRANT

would accept the immigrant if he were invisible and silent, but once a certain demographic density has been reached, the ghost assumes a terrifying consistency. To make matters worse, reassured by his growing numbers, he dares, on the contrary, to talk out loud in his native tongue and sometimes appears in his native dress. It is no easy thing to live with a bad conscience or feel historically beaten; at the very least it is difficult to reason calmly. Which leads to the astonishing confusion that arises when the problems of decolonization are raised.

A New Refrain

At some point it will be necessary to describe and evaluate the sequel to decolonization, but this time as it affects the French national. The so-called "*sans-papiers*" affair illustrates this new refrain, which has insinuated itself, for better or worse, between the two former partners in colonization. For the former colonist the situation should be marked "paid in full," as they say in business when a transaction is concluded. For the formerly colonized subject there is always some liability involved ("They've stolen enough from us! Now they owe us compensation!"). In this case the compensation is work and papers that allow one to work without doing so in fear. The immigrant who stages a sit-in inside a church, under the benevolent eye of the priest, and to the embarrassment of the archbishop, doesn't have the impression that he's committing an act that is especially scandalous or illegal. On the contrary, he feels he is being partially reimbursed for a debt that was formerly contracted. The feeling is quite widespread back home. "We didn't ask them for visas when they wanted to come here." Brazil, the most powerful country in South America, has still not forgotten that it was colonized

THE IMMIGRANT

by Portugal, which, apparently, is still obligated to show it preferential treatment. This opinion is held, more or less confusedly, by a segment of the Portuguese population, who support their claims. The unconditional defenders of illegal immigrants remember, for example, their contributions to the wars of the French Republic and the work of reconstruction that followed. "We owe it to them!" National identity papers should be issued to all immigrants, since this would enable them to escape their unbearable clandestine existence and, at the same time, give them the right to vote, without requiring naturalization; that is, they would no longer be considered wholly as foreigners. And certainly, in observing the fate of these exiles in their midst, their difficulties in getting here, the dangers involved, their stubbornness in reaching the host country in spite of the death of so many, the daily suffering, the permanent anxiety, the humiliation, it would be inhuman to refuse to help them improve their fate. It's difficult not to get carried away by one's emotions.

Yet it is also true, as another writer believes, that in doing so one contravenes current law. It means denying the concept of territory and national borders. It encourages and rewards the boldest. Issuing papers to anyone who asks means accepting the presence on one's home soil of any foreigner who asks. What then becomes of the nation? Who can predict the consequences of such an uncontrolled influx of people from a different land on the national culture, on institutions, the economy, demography? Doesn't this contribute to the decline of an already threatened Christian civilization? The uneasiness is more or less justified, and it coexists with a sense of anxiety on the part of the majority of the population, which will be reflected in its votes for increasingly right-wing candidates.

So, should we close our borders? Refuse to tolerate the

stratagems of the immigrants who are already here, which are easily identified, especially in small communities — the marriages of convenience, the fictional jobs from friends, the temporary lodgings. But this is where things get complicated. For the former colonial society needs immigrants, not only for the labor market but also demographically (the two are related). This carries considerable weight. Europe's population is aging rapidly. In four out of ten European countries, there are more deaths than births. This is not yet the case in the United States, which partly explains its behavior. How can these countries continue to fund retirement plans, which, although the policy is questionable, are paid for with taxes from younger members of the population? Aside from the reigning hypocrisy and the electoral cowardice of politicians in clearly exposing the situation, the equation is obvious: European women, legitimately interested in careers that had traditionally been reserved for men, are not reproducing fast enough to compensate for the demographic loss and the needs of production. Businesses were the — discreet — promoters of the first waves of immigration, supplying the workers they needed at low cost and putting pressure on the local proletariat. The first Algerians arriving in France in 1905 were called in to break a strike by the dockworkers in Marseilles. European industry no longer seems able to function without immigrant labor. Yet, in contrast to this need, the third world is populated with unoccupied young people, who attack Europe's battlements, turning it into a besieged fortress. But, as history teaches, no fortress can withstand an assault forever. Moreover, and quite unexpectedly, this fortress must — at least to some extent — maintain relations with its attackers, because it needs them. This is the source of considerable bewilderment for the host country.

Thus the dilemma of the ex-colonized corresponds to the

dilemma of the ex-colonizer who, having lost his colonies, hopes at least to be rid of a cumbersome weight. Now he assumes another role. Now he must address new problems, which he does not know how to resolve. For the former colonizer the question is how best to integrate the new arrivals. This isn't the first time the country has had to absorb an immigrant population—there were Polish miners, without whom the coal mines would have closed, Italian, Portuguese, and later, Spanish, masons. But these were individuals or small minorities, similar cultures with the same religion who ultimately assimilated and disappeared. The new immigrants compose large, compact groups with a different religion and different customs. How can they be integrated? And at what price? During the colonization of Algeria, some farsighted intellects realized that the only way to prevent upheavals among the colonized would be to make them loyal citizens of France. To which General de Gaulle remarked jokingly that, in that case, there would be several dozen Muslim *députés* in the National Assembly—something he found as unbearable as the majority of the French at the time. For what would become of the relative unity and identity of the nation? Fifty years later, in one of those ironies history supplies, the French, who preferred to abandon their colonies rather than jeopardize their national identity, find themselves facing the same problem. Immigration is the punishment for colonial sin.

What can the immigrant do in the face of this wall of scorn and suspicion? He reacts like any organism in a hostile environment. Through a natural reflex he protects himself, withdraws into himself, and turns to his friends; he will cling increasingly to the differences he is asked to renounce. The need for integration with the dominant group is felt as an unbearable constraint, a betrayal of his community of origin. Naturally, he doesn't regret having left and doesn't dream,

THE IMMIGRANT

at least for now, of returning. He has finally found a job, he's earning more than he ever did, there are plenty of ways to enjoy himself, legal and illegal, he has infinitely more freedom. But thinking he had crossed from purgatory to paradise, he discovers that he has moved from one purgatory to another, one that is more comfortable, to be sure, but one to whose laws he must submit. From now on, rather than simply demanding the new and complete citizenship so often talked about, he will keep his distance. He is expected to be transparent; on the contrary, he will become more opaque, he will become part of the ghetto.

The Ghetto

The ghetto is not only a substitute for the illusory promised land, but a mitigated form of the abandoned homeland. It is between these two representations that the immigrant's new, uprooted, life will unfold. In the small back alleys of the ghetto are places of worship, where exotic imams exhort their followers to respect the Koran and maintain solidarity with other Muslims. There are sympathetic cafés, where while drinking tea or playing the pinball machines, watching a North African, Egyptian, or Saudi Arabian television station, events are discussed, shared hopes and fears are aired, and rumors are exchanged. There are butcher shops with signs in Arabic characters, selling ritual, or "hallal," cuts of meat. With all the disorder of the souk, grocers sell the foods one ate as a child, the imported spices, grains, vegetables, and fruits, the displays overflowing into the street. There are five-and-dimes where one can find a motley assortment of prayer rugs, slippers, and plastic kitchen utensils. Here, guarded from the gaze of strangers, the immigrant does not feel like an outsider. Surrounded by familiar faces, even unknown, he almost feels at home, in the midst of a factitious majority. His home is what one would expect in this ghetto: cushions covered with brightly colored fabrics, rugs from home or mediocre Chinese copies, a tea service in chiseled copper imported from some Eastern country sitting on a pedestal table of imitation marquetry, a reproduction of the Kaaba, the black stone of Mecca, surrounded by countless throngs of pilgrims, a verse from the Koran above the entranceway. The apartment is small and odors from the tiny kitchen invade all the available space. On the window sill or the roof sits a satellite dish that indicates his belonging, far more than his name on a mailbox, and connects him to his "brothers" throughout the world. So, waiting for the, mythic, return to the homeland, which he speaks of so nonchalantly, he has created a facsimile that allows him to dream, and wait.

It is this concentration, both physical and cultural, that the majority, especially in France, designate, fear, and denounce as sectarianism. Suggesting, in their indignant suspicion, that it simply proves the immigrant's reluctance to become a part of the collective body of the nation. While not false, this is far from the complete picture. As often, the truth is circular. This ghetto is both a rejection and a reaction to rejection, real or imagined, by the others. The ghetto, like the former Jewish ghettos, supports and feeds the separation, but it is also its expression. It is the shell secreted by a minority group that feels, rightly or wrongly, that its very existence is threatened. To escape this threat the immigrant turns to his own, encloses himself within their embrace, in which he believes he is safe.

The formation of small communities within the nation is not the result of some perverse intent to destroy it, nor is it a philosophy. It is a spontaneous and utilitarian agglomeration of minorities unable to completely identify with the

THE IMMIGRANT

surrounding majority, which they simultaneously aspire to. This community enables them to better address, and possibly resolve, their specific problems, which the national community has difficulty resolving or refuses to consider. These include religious beliefs and political loyalties that do not necessarily coincide with those of their fellow citizens and which exile in fact helps to affirm, for without them their identity might be called into question. Those who follow Ramadan, however listlessly, believe they are required to fast consistently, at least out of solidarity. It's easy to see why fundamentalists are partial to the ghetto, for it is there that the collective personality has the greatest chance of survival. It is in the ghetto that their efforts at agitation can be maintained over the long term, an agitation that lends itself to their objectives.

However, the immigrant soon discovers that the ghetto is not the solution to his torment. The ghetto is a refuge, not a prison or confined space. He comes and goes for work, for amusement, for bureaucratic red tape. For better or worse he is required to confront this outside world, which increasingly becomes a part of him, to compare what he was to what he has become. The ghetto does not resolve any of the problems presented by the interactions between these two worlds. Sometimes a crisis erupts, triggered by an irresolvable contradiction, such as reconciling the importance of religion in Muslim life and republican secularism, or the ways in which the condition of women is addressed. The immigrant cannot demand equality and reject the conditions of integration.

Still, whether he wants it or not, regardless of the doubts of the majority, his integration in the surrounding society, along with his family and children, advances. The young among the Arab crowds demonstrating against America wear American baseball hats and jeans. Literature provides a range of

85

insights. There are a large number of works that attempt to describe the difficulties and contradictions of integration: the nostalgia for a homeland, the affirmation of an original identity, and the remonstrative, often guilty, wish for a more complete acceptance by the host country.

One never asserts one's identity so much as when it's threatened. It is when the Arab world is attempting to penetrate the community of nations that it discovers there is a price to pay. It is both fascinated by the Western world, whose victory, if not superiority, it tacitly recognizes, and repelled by the necessary abandonment of large swaths of tradition and collective personality. How could the immigrant do anything but live in a state of permanent crisis?

Head Scarves and *Métissage*

Like disease, crises are often productive; by exaggerating certain characteristics, they reveal the true nature of the organism. The issue of head scarves is instructive in this regard. We already know that these can signify a customary submission to an ethnic-religious tradition, like the cross worn by Catholics, the Protestant dove, the Jewish yarmulke, nothing more than sartorial conformity. My grandmother, who was not Muslim, would never go outside without being covered in her *haik*, the large piece of white fabric that covered her entire body, not just her head. We used to joke that she was "dressing up like a ghost." The events that shook the Arab-Muslim world, especially the wars against Iraq, have revealed other aspects of this situation. New wearers began to appear, who had never worn a head scarf previously. Their arguments, some weak, some clever, often had to do with freedom. For example, "We're free in France, aren't we? So, I'm free to wear a head scarf, right?" It is a foolish argument. For they fail to see that they

THE IMMIGRANT

are acting against their own interests in rejecting the laws that freed them in favor of the dogmas that enslaved them. In the name of a poorly understood secularism, they demand not to be secular. Moreover, the problem is not one of freedom but its signification. "The head scarf protects women from men's stares," they say. Why not also protect men from the stares of women? Aren't we showing favoritism to the female sex? To protect them from men's desire, is it necessary that they be undesirable, like those Orthodox Jewish women who shave their head? What's more, respecting those who wish to be protected in this way does not give you the right to criticize those who do not wish to be so protected. The religious argument also fails. "God demands it!" God gets blamed for a lot, it seems. What does divinity have to do with what is essentially a question of sex, and why should God privilege men? The Koran makes only a brief allusion to this issue, and it's no more than a suggestion. Even if wearing the head scarf were a kind of freedom for some, it should not be transformed into a requirement for all, which fundamentalists insist upon. Like excision, wearing a head scarf is a way of controlling women's bodies. Those women who recently began wearing it are participating in a regressive movement that has touched the Muslim world; they are turning their backs on women's freedom. They continue to subject themselves to the gnawing anxiety of men whenever their sexual privileges enter the picture. First in Algeria, then in other Western cities, masses of women have demonstrated in favor of wearing the head scarf. We are witnessing a return to bodily concealment in countries like Tunisia, where it had nearly disappeared—under pressure, it is true, from the authorities. It is as if women in the Middle Ages had asked to wear chastity belts. But underlying the arguments we find an element of protest, if not downright provocation: the head scarf has become the flag of

THE IMMIGRANT

a cause. "You don't like Muslims, the sight of them irritates you? Well, I'm proclaiming my Muslimhood; I'm forcing you to see it. To see a member of a group you have made to feel ashamed." What do you do when someone rejects your gesture of reconciliation? The head scarf is a portable ghetto, revealing a sense of discomfort about one's identity that affects Muslim immigrants. It's a way of strengthening an uncertain identity by enabling the wearer to distance herself from the majority.

This explains the embarrassment of the legislator and the man in the street, no matter how liberal: Should we see in this an adolescent passion for self-expression? Or a militant gesture, the first signs of an escalating battle? After the head scarf, what will they be asking for next! Haven't they already begun questioning the fundamental laws of the Republic: equality of the sexes, access to medical care, educational neutrality? The head scarf appears to be an element of a more general form of behavior, the defensive and offensive recourse to another tradition. Thus considered, the head scarf, like the consumption of ritually prepared meat or the observance of Ramadan, is part of the machinery of survival of the Muslim community, submerged in a Christian or, worse still, irreligious universe. This helps explain the vehemence that accompanies debate on this topic, revealing the underlying and reciprocal anxiety involved.

Yet, regardless of their anxiety, the majority of immigrants are strongly tempted by integration, which is the exactly opposite solution. Yet, it is no easier. For in the end it leads to intermarriage, the risk of dilution within the majority population. Once again this causes embarrassment for Arab intellectuals, whose involvement in what might have been a rewarding debate has been minimal: what role should the adoption of Western, that is, European, values play in the future of

THE IMMIGRANT

Arab societies? It is possible that, had they been consulted, a majority would have been in favor of wearing head scarves. Even if intermarriage is the likely future of our mobile societies, it continues to generate fear. Yet here too we would benefit from clearly exposing the risks involved, a discussion intellectuals should contribute to.

In this respect, mixed marriages have much to teach us. It is estimated that 50 percent of young French Jews intermarry, although condemned by the rabbinical authorities, who see themselves as the guardians of the Jewish community. We don't have figures for young French Arabs but it's probably not much different. Arab leaders urge the conversion of the non-Muslim spouse, which has the advantage of enriching the group with a new member. Similarly, the Catholic church tolerates mixed marriages providing the children are baptized. For the moment, mixed marriage is seen almost as a form of treason; no group willingly consents to what appears to it a form of suicide.

In short, there is no perfect solution for minorities; assimilation has never been convenient, at least in the beginning. The spouse in a mixed marriage must confront the possible contradictions between his group of origin and the host group. How can a Jewish believer easily accept working on Saturday? A Muslim believer accept eating pork in the cafeteria? They hesitate between greater strictness, if not isolation, which separates them even more from their newfound peers, or dilution and possibly collective disappearance. Moreover, since not everyone is gifted with a sense of cosmopolitanism and its potential consequences, marital problems or even separation are more common in mixed marriages than in others.

THE IMMIGRANT

Humiliation

The end of colonization, a place in international organizations following the emergence of independent nations, petrodollars, participation in banking systems, the considerable enrichment of some, and an increasingly obvious sense of cultural and religious affirmation—these are some of the things that have given hope to the Arab-Muslim world that a new era is dawning. However, it is not always convenient to be Arab, or black, in the West. On the contrary, the greater proximity to the world's economic and political affairs, the presence of a diversified labor environment, and the social role of women have painfully highlighted the gap that continues to exist between the former masters and the liberated. The feeling of inequality, having become intolerable, nourishes a growing bitterness. The presence of increasingly greater numbers of immigrants in the West itself reflects a new expansion of Islam, but also its continued defeat, its inability to satisfy its young. Such frustration provides fertile ground, is an argument for, Islamic activism. To force complete equality with the perverse and egotistical West, preoccupied solely with its privileges, a bitter struggle is needed, war.

However, it is not obvious that activists could conduct a real war. For war to be possible, both adversaries would have to be relatively equal; but until now the ex-colonized have not succeeded in achieving the same ranking as the West, as they say in the world of sports. There is no way to overcome this. Even taking into account a relative decline, the West retains considerable superiority—scientific, technical, military, even philosophical. It is the West's conception of the universe, strongly inspired by advances in science, and its universalist morality that govern, for better or worse, the relations between inhabitants of the planet. The theory of

THE IMMIGRANT

human rights, for example, although it has become a stereotype, is acknowledged, although grudgingly, even hypocritically, by the majority of thinking people around the world. To which the third world can only reply with thinkers who are no longer relevant; Averroës and Maimonides date from the twelfth century. Since then, Freud, Marx, and Einstein have guided our thinking. Brilliant individuals, increasingly numerous, are making a career for themselves in laboratories and universities, but they use Western science and technology. Strict fundamentalists do not dismiss planes, trains, and cell phones, which have proved to be useful in conquering space and time. Until now, every military battle against the West has been lost. One of history's ironies is that Kosovo, a Muslim territory, owes its survival to the assistance of the Americans, just as Nasser's pseudo-victory against France, England, and Israel was obtained through the intervention of the Americans and Russians.

The war between the third world and the West has therefore been reduced to single operations, conducted by small groups or individuals, champions who are sacrificed specifically to avoid direct confrontation. But the attacks and car bombs, while they result in individual suffering and terrible destruction, can never achieve decisive results. Although they provide a form of vengeful satisfaction, they also increase the painful feeling of collective impotence.

It is has been asked if all the ex-colonized experience this feeling of humiliation, arising from a constant shared sense of defeat, and the hope that they will be released by some unforeseen event—a theory supported by fundamentalist activists. A Muslim intellectual has gone so far as to say that in every Muslim there is a sleeping fundamentalist. As long as he's asleep, things are not so bad. Any totalization is a mistake and unjust, but there are objective conditions that force

91

THE IMMIGRANT

themselves upon nearly all members of a group. Even though they deny it or are not fully conscious of it, they are aware of it in their thoughts and in their actions. There is also a female condition that every woman experiences, even when fate or the accidents of birth enable her to avoid it. There is a Jewish condition as well, which the Jew can accept or reject. After being colonized, the decolonized must confront a new situation to which, even though he is not individually affected, he must respond—according to his temperament and social affiliations—through subterfuge, resignation, or revolt. What does he see, when walking in the street, other than the signs of his own people's inferiority? The street sweepers, laborers, and sewer workers are almost all immigrants; as if the slavery of old had simply changed its physiognomy. "I will rip the *Banania* smiles off all the walls of France," promised Léopold Sédar Senghor. *Banania*'s Negro is now nowhere to be seen on walls, but he is in the streets. Only he no longer wears that brilliant smile. The difficulty of finding an apartment, and employment and sexual discrimination, have led to bitterness. Although he may manage to overcome such difficulties in his own life, poverty and exclusion by the majority contribute to the humiliation of his peers. How many in the majority community spend time with immigrants, invite them home, or willingly visit their homes? Whether he sells chestnuts illegally on the street or manages a supermarket, the immigrant never feels he is a legitimate citizen in his new country.

Who is to blame? The response is not as simple as it might seem. It cannot be placed on the refusal of the majority alone. The immigrants' life and their relations with the national population are both governed by objective mechanisms. The immigrant is a newcomer, and latecomers rarely get the best seats in the house—especially when there exists a misunderstanding between the majority and the immigrant. The

92

THE IMMIGRANT

immigrant is in a hurry to obtain the same status as his new fellow citizens; why doesn't he have access to the best jobs, for example? But the majority feels that it has already given the immigrant quite a lot by simply accepting him. It cannot, from the outset, offer him all the advantages that accrue to those with roots in the society; he has to prove himself. In the meanwhile, it asks that he be recognizant and, at least, comply with the customs of society. It is up to the immigrant to blend in with the national community. And certainly that is the wisest course to follow in a foreign land. But the hesitations of the majority cause the immigrant to hesitate. Now he is asked to pile failure upon failure. The first was the decision to quit the homeland; now they have upped the ante: he must change his beliefs or pretend to do so. Confronted with this dilemma, the immigrant feels himself teetering dizzily over the edge of an abyss. "Without my turban I feel naked," a Pakistani immigrant lamented.

How could the majority comprehend the reticence, the reluctance of its guest, for whom, in spite of everything, they have, with generosity as far as they are concerned, opened their doors? The imposition of their laws and customs is legitimate, naturally, because they are part of the air they breathe. Even if they don't attend church regularly, their existence is governed by religious traditions, their holidays are fundamentally religious in nature, the children's vacations coincide with the clerical calendar; their national celebrations, even though they joke about them, are an intimate part of the culture; the city is spattered with monuments to their collective memory. The majority experiences a kind of spontaneous myopia that prevents them from seeing the minorities that live among them. How could the insistent presence of the immigrant not appear unusual, almost threatening, to an equilibrium it has taken centuries to establish? A colleague of mine, who could hardly be suspected of racism or xenophobia, confided that "A black crime novel felt out of place to me." He no longer recognized the characters he was accustomed to reading about. Many in the majority are less comfortable in the presence of an immigrant doctor, just as an immigrant prefers to visit a doctor from his own country. Thus the integration everyone talks about as a necessity, without knowing exactly what it is, is both desired and rejected by both parties.

From Humiliation to Resentment

We need to realize that a sense of profound resentment runs through the ex–third world and, more specifically, the Arab world. It has always existed but can now express itself openly. This is the resentment of the conquered, who see no obvious outlet for their defeat. The violence of this movement is so considerable because the third world is greatly dependent on the West while the West has little need of the third world. We could do without coffee harvested in Africa or Central America but not the drugs developed in European laboratories. The third world draws extensively from Western culture. The West, aside from a handful of borrowings — musical rhythms and clothing—borrows little from the third world. There is a sad irony in the fact that, having reconquered the right to live out its singularity, the third world must borrow so much from others. It has always been this way between oppressor and oppressed; the culture of the oppressor goes hand in hand with its economic and political power. True, there are oil and certain raw materials, but these can always be obtained with cash. The third world has greater need to sell its oil than the West to buy it, for this is the greatest source of its income . . . income that it reinvests in Western economies.

What are the alternatives when one is beaten down and

THE IMMIGRANT

humiliated by defeat? Dream of a better life? Of a nostalgic past when one was powerful and rich, wise and cultivated, with mythical ancestors, superhuman heroes, kings ruling over immense empires? Of a fabulous future, when one will again be rich and prosperous and invincible? But the gap between the ideal life and reality does not favor a sense of equilibrium and self-control. The reality one experiences in everyday life and that constitutes one's ordinary experience is one of interminable convalescence from the consequences of colonization, widespread poverty, and the scandalous wealth of a small minority, the corruption of the haves and the petty bribes of the majority. There is a sense of mass resignation in spite of the sporadic disorderly, ineffective, and easily repressed outbreaks, the refusal of responsibility or complicity of the elites, the diminishment of culture to the benefit of religious obscurantism, the motivated and derisive plotting associated with politics, the envious comparisons (almost always detrimental) with other peoples, some of whom, less gifted by nature, nevertheless manage to succeed in their development.

The decolonized could also approach his wants with a more lucid eye, evaluate his own share of responsibility. Some authors have had the courage to do this. But such meritorious self-criticism does not eliminate the guilt and the pain, not to mention the indignation of his peers in the face of what are felt to be such untimely revelations. During the second Anglo-American war against Iraq, the Baghdad national museum, which contained precious artifacts for understanding the heritage of humanity, was pillaged and vandalized. There was an uproar of accusation by the Iraqis, which was broadly circulated in the European press: the Americans had orchestrated the calamity. "They wanted to steal our memory!" This was the accusation of the Baghdad residents interviewed, and was spoken with tears in their eyes. What benefit would

THE IMMIGRANT

the Americans have obtained from stealing the collective memory of the Iraqi people? In what sense, for that matter, are Chaldea and Sumer part of Arab memory, a people who, at the time, existed as no more than a handful of tribes in the Arabian Peninsula? Shortly after, it was discovered that the thieves were Iraqi traffickers, similar to the Egyptian tomb robbers of old, who lived off their fruitful trade, and the traffickers of the treasures of the temples of Angkor (one of whom was André Malraux). The bubble burst. But the same journalists who were so quick to describe with horror the so-called sacrilege committed by the occupation forces changed their tune: the Americans hadn't carried off the famous vases and bas-reliefs, but they had let it happen. They were, all the same, the real guilty party. After some more time elapsed, it was learned that the principal artworks, which were thought to have disappeared, had been saved by an alert employee and hidden in the museum's basement. The crime never happened. The affair was, however, rich with insight: the Iraqis were exculpated and the others were found guilty. Most likely this dénouement will be forgotten and the only thing remembered will be the criminal negligence of the Americans.

This transfer of responsibility results in victimization, which absolves or alleges collective guilt, stigmatizes a guilty party from outside the community, and, at the same time, builds resentment. During every crisis, when violence occurs, the participants never ask themselves the role they each play in the event, the possible strategy of their rulers. With one voice the Arab world shouts, "We're being attacked! They're trying to destroy us!" As if a universal plot against them were afoot, without any involvement at all on the part of the Arab world. Throughout the Iraq war, questionable as it may be, Arab commentators have been silent about the crimes of Saddam Hussein and his regime; the war is seen as an attack against the entire Arab world. Even in peacetime, Arab activists, more or less confusedly followed by public opinion, feel they have been despoiled by the rest of the universe. "They've excluded us from the world's banquet!" writes one of their poets. Why, we may ask, don't they organize their own banquets? Because that would mean recognizing their own personal failings, and to accuse oneself means recognizing—more or less—that one is guilty. It is easier to blame others, all the others, since they can be treated as one.

It follows that resentment encompasses all non-Muslims throughout the world, at the very least throughout the West. If the hatred of America has replaced that of the colonizer, it's not only because the United States represents the stronger party, it's because it is the quintessence of the West. Therefore, it will be hit first. But no one in the West is innocent when it comes to the misfortune of the Arab people. They all deserve to be punished to varying degrees, even their descendants. This is a negative debt that they will all have to pay, sooner or later. Like resentment, vengeance is totalizing. And it is not enough to point a finger at the guilty; they must be punished, that is, symbolically destroyed. We see in the majority of trials that this is the price to be paid to reestablish the integrity of the victim. An additional benefit is that resentment and vengeance provide an opportunity to achieve a more close-knit communion among the victims, now wedded in their distress and their eventual victory.

But, as fate would have it, resentment is still an expression of dependence. And to the extent that activists benefit from the indulgence of the populace, the life of the ex-colonized is marked by what is far from a minor contradiction: its activists desire, and believe they can bring about, the destruction of a society, in which they hope, in spite of everything, to find a place.

THE IMMIGRANT

The Solidarity of the Vanquished

The current collision—there have been others—between the Arab-Muslim world and the West has two sides: violence and solidarity. Violence against the West and unconditional solidarity among Arabs. The unconditional solidarity is the reaction of the vanquished and oppressed. The conquerors have no need of it, they are sufficient unto themselves. Thus, solidarity among Jews is more accentuated than that found in the majority of the population because they feel permanently threatened. We find solidarity among blacks because of the handicap of color that inevitably brings them to the attention of others. There is an instinctive solidarity among women because of their fragility in the face of masculine endeavors. The solidarity of the colonized is still alive among the decolonized.

First, there is the spontaneous emotional solidarity that leads us to run to the aid of a compatriot whenever we sense he is in danger. With respect to the fate of the Palestinians, an intellectual confided, "Sometimes I can't sleep. . . . I start to cry." But there is also selective solidarity. Out of discretion I didn't ask if her sleep was disturbed during the wars among Arabs, or when the Kurds were gassed by the Iraqis. She did not cry during the war between Iran and Iraq, when Iraq, an Arab country, was the assailant, nor during the destruction of passenger aircraft by Khadafi's henchmen—an involvement Khadafi ultimately acknowledged. But the injustice toward the Palestinians is something that affects her personally, not the Kurds, since they are the victims of other Arabs. There were no angry crowds or even any protest marches, for that matter. During the conflict between Greece and Turkey, a psychiatrist friend, a man professionally capable of logic and rationality, politically liberal, told me that he

98

THE IMMIGRANT

had "flipped." "I no longer knew where I was." His reason advised him, until additional information was available, to maintain a sense of balance between the two adversaries, but his heart went out to Turkey, a nation that is not Arab but is nonetheless Muslim.

Solidarity automatically generates indulgence. The same people who recoil in fear at the attacks perpetrated by suicide bombers or condemn them outright ("They're insane!") believe that bin Laden is a symbol, a kind of hero. At the same time, they feel he's full of himself. The evidence notwithstanding, there is a kind of instinctive sympathy if not admiration for heroes even though they are not above reproach. Those who saw that Saddam Hussein was a horrible tyrant were still opposed to the steps taken to oust him, first the sanctions and then the war. In their defense, they note that international laws have been violated by the Americans—which is true enough for the second Iraq war but not for the first, which received the approval of the United Nations and most nations. It is not so much a question of respecting international law, which is ineffective enough to begin with, and for which they were not so concerned on other occasions, as preventing aggression against a brother country. In any case, they are glad to have held high their shared colors against the West.

Solidarity has transformed itself into an imperious duty that transcends the law, which is perceived as a creation of the West to serve its own interests, a not inaccurate statement. Activists do not fail to remind the weak of this, sometimes forcefully. Moderate Arab regimes will be punished along with the infidels. There exists a kind of objective responsibility that is imposed on all Muslims in the face of the immoral condition facing them: whoever withdraws from the fight is considered a traitor, for he is playing into the enemy's hands. Yet, even a simple statement, an allusion, or doubt weakens

THE IMMIGRANT

this joint offensive. Anyone who carefully maintains this inevitable connection is considered a saint. If he gives his life, he is considered a martyr, the expression of the highest form of virtue, since he has sacrificed himself for the sake of the community. Whether through bravado or provocation, mothers proclaim their sense of pride in sacrificing their children. The names of suicide bombers are regularly followed by the word *shahid,* or martyr. Is it onomastic coincidence that gave the name Leila *Shahid*—whose real name was Shahed—to the official representative of Palestine in France or the sign of her solidarity with suicide bombers?

Of course, solidarity in itself is not negative. It supports the individual and strengthens the social bond, creates a euphoric feeling of communion. It provides a measure of protection against the real or imagined hostility of those outside the group, and it provides help to the poor and rights wrongs. But it becomes unjust whenever it is unconditional. Emotional outbreaks are not conducive to a rational examination of events; they engender collective fantasies, veil the truth, and lead to sectarian behavior. It is not about knowing who is right and who is wrong, but strongly resembles such judgment. The legitimate struggle against the injustice suffered by Muslims thus results in perpetrating injustice against non-Muslims. The same was true of the Christian Middle Ages. The testimony of a Muslim before the law is supposed to carry more weight than that of a nonbeliever. This unfairness has not yet entirely disappeared, for example, with respect to minorities who live in Islamic countries. It leads to the conclusion that the Arab-Muslim world is monolithic, which is not the case. It is not true that all Muslims today feel that a thief's hand should be cut off or that adulterous women should be stoned to death. But their condemnation is not subject to the full light of day, it remains masked by the demands

THE IMMIGRANT

of solidarity; so that the debate is confined to the Arab world, between those who hold to tradition and those who wish to confront modernity. In terms of diplomacy, the automatic majorities that follow from unconditional solidarity in international assemblies have ruined their credibility. General de Gaulle, speaking at the United Nations, referred to this solidarity as "bogus," and a diplomat remarked that they could carry a vote even after having claimed to square the circle. In 2003, Colonel Khadafi, dictator for life, succeeded in getting one of his men elected as the head of the human rights commission: all the Arab states voted for him. Unconditional solidarity prevents the emergence of any true international law, which is not simply a compromise among national egos. Certainly, the Arabs are not the only ones responsible, but they are also not among those trying to build a sense of universal morality. Adopting such a stance often works against them. Whatever the advantages of solidarity, don't these individual states have an interest in promoting a form of shared justice?

Composite Identity

Unconditional solidarity requires a kind of systematic apology. Those who express shock at the presence of eunuchs in nearly all Arab courts until the modern era, are informed that castration is forbidden by Islam. The dialogue generally goes something like this: "Yes, but that doesn't prevent the use of eunuchs, at least to guard the harems." "True, but the Arabs only bought them from 'castrato factories,' and those most often belonged to oriental Christians. Moreover, the Roman Catholic Church also purchased eunuchs to sing their ritual chants as late as the seventeenth century."

So, if the Arabs only purchased them, they have to be absolved? Does one crime excuse another? The injunction

THE IMMIGRANT

against usury among Muslims as well as Christians has in no way prevented true believers from taking advantage of it when needed, placing the blame on the Jewish lender.

What happens when you allude to the tragedy of black slavery, organized by Arab merchants, who made expeditions to the heart of Africa, who gathered large numbers of men, women, and even children, many of whom died on the way to the holds of the ships that transported them?

You are told that the Arabs were content to sell them to Europeans, Christians, who made them slaves for the needs of the American colonies. What's more, there was complicity on the part of some traditional African leaders. Therefore, if the Arabs limited themselves to supplying the slave traders, with the help of the blacks themselves, then they must be absolved. QED.

They argue that those crimes must be placed in the context of an age when castration and slavery were socially accepted. So be it. But we are not talking only of the past. Castration is still practiced; slavery is still in use in Saudi Arabia, the Sudan, Mauritania, Yemen, the Emirates. In Bamako (Mali), the rulers, former students of the great European, Russian, and American institutions, upon their return home, naturally found their slaves waiting for them. The beys of Tunis, tiny kinglets whose power depended on the Ottoman Empire, had slaves and eunuchs until the abolition of the monarchy by Bourguiba, a few decades ago. In Algeria, a black slave market was active in Aflou on the high plateaux. Why did a democratic Algeria tolerate its existence? Why did it not speak out against the persistence of such abominable practices? Why, today, through its silence, does the Arab community seem to approve of excision, a form of mutilation that deprives young women of their sexuality and endangers their life? After it was banned by the French government, parents residing in France

102

THE IMMIGRANT

sent their young daughters back home to be cut. There have been no protests to date among the Arab community, nor, for that matter, from European intellectuals. They gently explain that the practice is a rite, surprising for Westerners but part of a "cultural context" that cannot be eliminated from one day to the next without affecting the entire culture. Or that young women who refuse to submit to the practice risk remaining unmarried, and so on. Therefore, out of respect (how many crimes have been committed in the name of respect for something?) . . . out of respect for a cultural practice, suffering, mutilation, and death are acceptable? Is it also acceptable that young musicians should have their eyes torn out so they can concentrate on their art because it was once customary?

The complaisance of the apologist, if not his bad faith, which is common, for that matter, to the guardians of all traditions, is boundless. At the World Islamic Conference, aside from a few Platonic regrets, with the exception of one or two voices, no head of state was willing to sign a resolution condemning suicide attacks. To justify the unjustifiable, the apologist twists the neck of truth and justice. He reverses values, praises fantasies of identity. A young woman, a professor, explained in all seriousness that Ramadan allowed people to lose weight safely. Belly dancing, a pleasant erotic diversion, has become the symbol of spirituality. Not long ago, a Muslim professor of theology who taught in virtuous Geneva, attempted to defend the lynching of women convicted of adultery. Would you prefer, he argued, the sexual laxity of the West? Only Islam is capable of serving as a rampart against such indecent behavior, which is liable to pollute the entire planet. Another, more innocent, makes an inventory of French words of Arabic origin: apricot, bazaar, magazine . . . or emphasizes the transmission of Greek philosophy to the West (which is true enough), wishing to reveal the extent

THE IMMIGRANT

of the West's debt to the East (which certainly exists), and even the superiority of the East (which goes without saying). "Haven't you oppressed us, belittled us, and robbed us enough already? We're going to show you that we are as good as you, even better, and that we can easily do without you!"

It is always a matter of defending the collective personality of one's people, unjustly criticized and threatened. The apologist is not wrong in this, however. Decolonization and liberation have also resulted in a direct confrontation between Western values and their own. But it is not obvious that the decolonized is up to meeting this historical challenge. Even when, through one form of sophistry or another, he transforms his weaknesses into advantages, at bottom he fears he is still a loser, as he was during the period of Western domination. Except for the most isolated desert regions, every culture is subject to such assault; every culture is dynamic and composite, in constant transformation, especially since the onset of globalization. Every identity becomes a site of conflict within itself and at variance with others. Even the civilization of the ex-colonizer clashes with that of the more vigorous American offshoot, which begins to overwhelm it. Nonetheless, the civilization retains enough stability to sustain such incursions, which tend rather to enrich it, and are often no more than decoration against a shared Western background.

Beneath its belligerent public face, fundamentalism, and the fanaticism that accompanies it, is the product of despair—the despair of those who are no match for the inevitable struggle. They can only reply with a return to a lost integrity, in other words, a retreat before the obstacles facing them. A return to what, though? Where is this pure integrity? What does it consist of? Aside from a handful of primal myths, whose interpretation varies depending on the school

104

THE IMMIGRANT

and the need, Arabic culture, as we know it today, is the result of the long and fruitful search of Arab conquerors among various conquered peoples. Islam took from Iran and Turkey as much as it gave. Today, those countries are a long way from the civilization of the Bedouins of Muhammad's time. Fundamentalism is an atavistic utopia, and to assume that this past really existed as they present it, fundamentalists use outdated weapons for a new conflict.

Whenever someone affirms his identity with such force, it is already endangered. Notwithstanding such statements of identity, Westernization, simultaneously embraced and deplored, has gradually impregnated the common heritage of all peoples. The younger generations, the children of immigrants, prefer rock to traditional *malouf;* this may reflect a lack of good taste, but they get the same pleasure from it as other young people around the world. It is easy to criticize snack food, but it is filling and adolescents can afford it. Powerful, wealthy Japanese businessmen who make business deals with Europeans do not show up for meetings in kimonos but in suits. Human rights have been irreversibly acquired by all peoples, even those who claim to reject them. It is in the name of such rights that we demand legal and humanitarian protections for the prisoners held at Guantánamo, who would like to destroy those same rights.

It is even possible that this new system of values has created a new, shared form of dependence. But its success is not accidental, for it tends toward a greater autonomy for individuals and peoples, an autonomy everyone now demands. This is not something necessarily easy to live out, however. For it may be easier to live isolated in one's village than to confront the world; easier to lock up women than to confront their sexuality and the mutual attraction of the sexes. Yet such gains are probably irreversible. The decolonized cannot reject

THE IMMIGRANT

them, as the fundamentalists demand, simply because, as history would have it, they have been proposed by the West. Besides, how would they go about it? Short of the Islamization of the West—something the mad imams in London cry out for—the decolonized, especially an immigrant, has no choice other than to live out the conflicts that arise from immersion in another culture. Like all inhabitants of the planet, his personality will be increasingly composite. It is true that this is more troubling for him because, if he wishes to access modernity, he must renounce part of what he was.

Abandoning the Myth of Return

The immigrant knows, for example, that aside from periodic visits of a tourist nature, he will never willingly return to his homeland. He is not far from thinking that this would, on the contrary, be a catastrophic upheaval in his life. He has discovered, and openly acknowledges, that the myth is over, the myth of a final return.

For a long time he wanted to believe that one day he would put an end to what he considered a form of exile. Not all those living in exile were colonial subjects, but all former colonial subjects now settled in a host country feel they are exiles. And then there are the voluntary exiles. This too is a rationalization, which exculpates the immigrant for abandoning his country. He can claim to have left because forced by poverty, especially the insupportable poverty of his family, to whom he can now send part of his salary on a regular basis. One day he will put an end to this situation, which separates him from his loved ones, without knowing exactly how. The time passes, he makes another life for himself, with its new routines and amusements, almost as true as the old one. Exile is not always misfortune. Some plants, when they are moved, wither

THE IMMIGRANT

and die, others adapt well and experience rapid growth. It is the return to the old country that becomes a kind of dream, gradually losing its substantiality. The only thing that remains for sure is nostalgia, and, after all, absence makes the heart grow fonder. It is as if his country had greater presence for him now than when he lived there. The Maghrebian tenderly evokes the summer evenings, the sea, the fresh and abundant fish purchased directly from the fisherman; the camel with its eyes shielded to prevent vertigo, turning ceaselessly around the noria to release health-bringing water from the depths of the earth. He praises the exquisite aromas of jasmine, orange flowers, and spices wafted on the breeze, forgetting the nauseating odor of garbage overlooked by a negligent municipality, the insistent rot from the lake into which the refuse of the city flows, supporting a fauna of large fat mullets, which are appreciated by everyone, rich and poor alike. He passes in silence the perfidy of the sun, the torpor of July and August, which burns lungs and vegetation, except for the luminous insolence of the hibiscus and the tenacious modesty of the geraniums, while he awaits the providential caesura of August 15, the feast of the Virgin, the Madonna of the Sicilians, which signals the start of the slow waning of the heat wave. Against a host country where, he claims, everything is harsh—the climate, the people, the customs—he continues to defend a homeland to which he insists he will one day return but which has become increasingly imaginary, whose continued survival the money he sends back helps maintain, like those carefully preserved ghost towns of Portuguese immigrants, where all the windows have curtains and every garage an automobile, but which will never be inhabited.

But while the home country has not changed, at least in his memory, he has been gradually transformed. Following a relaxation of legislation in the host country, his wife has

107

THE IMMIGRANT

been able to join him. He's no longer a bachelor wandering the sidewalks near the Barbès train station in Paris, between the apartment he shares with a roommate and the café where he meets his friends, not knowing what to do with himself. Those who have never known the solitude of exile cannot understand the sense of abandonment and bitterness; the first waves of immigrants were almost all bachelors. The new law, which allows family members to emigrate, has saved him from his mute despair. The host country is not the anticipated paradise, naturally, but there's work, a roof over his head, welfare laws (!) that no one can challenge, except for a horrid racist minority, themselves condemned by the majority of the population. He gets free health care and he's properly dressed. Now he's reunited with his wife, whose blessed hands provide him with the foods he remembers from childhood. He knows how to navigate the system, as does his wife, who regularly exchanges information with her friends. They receive a housing allocation, which pays for nearly all their rent, a travel discount that allows them to travel almost for nothing, a guarantee of a minimum income if he's already been employed, unemployment compensation, even if he's never held down a legal job, a "family" allocation, complete health care coverage. His wife receives a stipend for staying at home, and there's even a stipend for single parents, if you get legally divorced, even when you continue to live together; sometimes there's a stipend for being a political refugee. If necessary, he will change his name. He'll need new papers for that, but there are any number of places that specialize in forged papers; the Cameroonais are reputed to be the best. If the government questions him, he will demand free legal aid from an attorney. Why do without? Besides, no one's really doing him a favor, all the French benefit from such services, so why not him, since he's poor?

THE IMMIGRANT

To his surprise he soon discovers that he has spent more time here than there (which is *here* and which is *there* now?). He still returns home periodically, less frequently since his wife joined him, but he realizes, with some embarrassment, that he is no longer as comfortable there as he thought he would be. He was an immigrant. Now he's been transformed into an exile in his own country. The language, for example, has changed in his absence. He doesn't understand some of the new words, born of new situations, especially among the young; and he is annoyed at the speed at which they speak. After a while he no longer dreams of returning; he navigates between his two nostalgias and distances himself from both, which is, after all, realistic.

If he has been smart enough to leave behind the schemes and poor jobs of years ago and open a small business, a grocery store, café, or garage, isn't he, at least economically, a citizen of the host country, where he pays taxes? Even if he doesn't take part in elections, that will come eventually. And when he returns home with a car full of gadgets, which he will sell for as much as he can get, in order to pay his and his wife's ship or plane tickets, isn't he simply doing business with his former countrymen, much as if they were foreigners? If he's an intellectual, he will continue to talk about "roots," to ask for a "return to the source," to defend his "identity," without going into too much detail about what sources and roots now mean. Yes, he had a satellite dish installed so he could be directly connected to the Arab countries, and even watches Al Jazeera, in which he has confidence, and which is a way for him to focus on his "Oriental" side. This is understandable when you're far away, but is paradoxical nonetheless since back home people are more familiar with the Western stations like France 2, as they try to escape the grip of the stifling local networks. In private he doesn't worry too much

THE IMMIGRANT

about ridiculing such "Orientals," who are backwards, after all, in spite of their fabulous wealth. How do their wives manage to eat with that veil over their face? Do they have to lift it up like the hood of a car? He doesn't approve of their rulers, who stay in power without free elections, often with the help of military power. He is disinterested in the fantasies of a bygone age, the stagnation of custom—isn't it said that in Black Africa cannibalism hasn't entirely disappeared? Of course, he's not going to abandon the traditional rituals, he would be afraid of losing his identity entirely, and then what would he be able to offer his children? Although an unquestioned duty, it's one he no longer identifies with completely. Although he doesn't deny his solidarity with the Arab populace, he fears the displays of violence. He's a bit ashamed of those Iranian flagellants who whip themselves ecstatically until they bleed. The suicide bombers, although he certainly understands their despair, give Islam a bad image in the world. Unquestionably, the society of those countries is still closed, with their old walls waiting to fall.

In short, how could he fail to recognize his adoption of the values of freedom and progress of Western nations: human rights and democracy, freedom of thought, justice for women—who, for that matter, don't bother to ask his advice, imitating Western women, like the wives of some of his friends—even a certain respect for minorities? After all, isn't he a minority? Following this train of thought, he wonders timidly if he might not struggle in one of the organizations that defend such values. He is already quite satisfied that the union supports him when professional issues and social benefits are at stake. He wonders which is the correct position to assume with respect to wearing head scarves or the question of the *sans-papiers*, who want—and without delay, even though they entered the host country illegally and refuse to

THE IMMIGRANT

ask for naturalization—what it took him so much effort to achieve. If he wasn't afraid to appear hesitant in showing his solidarity with other Arabs around the world, he would say, "After all, I'm a French Muslim, a citizen like the rest of them. . . . if the others are willing to accept me." This will eventually happen, in spite of his accent, his face, and the oddity of his name.

No, without question, he won't return. He'll grow old here, like those old laborers of years ago, the *chibanis*, who refused to leave, even when their family back home urged them to, as if they were suggesting that they come home to die among them. You can see them, walking two or three abreast, berets on their heads, like so many working-class Frenchmen, or conversing on a bench not far from where they live. But they are like old slaves who have been freed, who can no longer even dream of freedom. The immigrant believes himself a free man, increasingly free. Is he still the same man who left his homeland so long ago? Yes, the churches have replaced the mosques and bells the call of the muezzin, but he can pray in one of the unused storefronts until something better comes along. Wasn't there talk of building a real mosque in the neighborhood? Naturally, with the arrival of his children, the situation changed. There was no going back.

The Immigrant's Son

There is a divide between the immigrant and his children. They don't share the same memories or the same idea of the future, they practically live in different worlds. The immigrant is, after all, a man of the past; his son and daughter are looking toward the future, even if they grow impatient, even if they despair of ever getting there, or refuse to do so. The immigrant's past, even when increasingly clouded by the fog

THE IMMIGRANT

of memory, provides him with a base, although increasingly fabricated, the object of his nostalgic yearning, a place he dreams of eventually returning to. In spite of everything, he still has relatives back home, and friends with whom he corresponds, talks to on the phone, stays with when he travels. He may even have an apartment of his own there. For his children there is no possible return since they never left; and when they do travel to their parents' home, everything is unfamiliar to them. It's not a return but a voyage of discovery, and often disappointing. The immigrant's vacation, a custom borrowed from the West, is synonymous with an obligatory stay back home; his son would just as well travel to Germany or Italy, where he may have a girlfriend. They do not really belong to the same community. The immigrant lives a double life that he tries to harmonize. The son, depending on his mood and the circumstance, asserts that he is French just as easily as he claims affiliation with Algeria, Morocco, or Tunisia. But in both cases he does so to provoke, to challenge the others, to convince himself, like those believers who, in the grip of self-doubt, recite a prayer to reaffirm the existence of God. The immigrant has more in common with the citizen who has remained behind than he does with his own children.

The immigrant does not even understand these young people, in spite of the fact that they are his. He had a goal, which he almost achieved. By reaching the host country he hoped to escape poverty and integrate as much as possible into the new society, mix with the inhabitants, all the while preserving his religion and a few marks of his own identity. Now he dresses like his fellow citizens, applies for the same jobs, enjoys the same entertainment, dreams of owning a car, sends his children to school with the other children, even though they are sometimes less diligent, which troubles him, for he knows that school is the gateway to advancement. His wife knows

THE IMMIGRANT

the local shops and stores and how to hunt for a bargain. If he could, he would willingly disappear into the crowd. But not only do his children disdain these acquisitions, they challenge them; they are outspoken, demanding, aggressive. He delights in the advantages obtained with such difficulty. But for them, they are never enough—"They gave us nothing!" they exclaim—as if such acquisitions were their inalienable right. Assimilation, the parents' desire and great hope, seems to have become instead a humiliating constraint for the children, when it is finally within their grasp. His daughters are even less recognizable. What sense of provocation leads them to cover their head when they know this draws attention? It's true that sometimes he's the one who demands this, which also leads them to rebel. One way or another they are always trying to escape the traditional expressions of parental authority. They scandalize him with their outrageous makeup and obscene miniskirts; they have relationships with boys, something he is shocked by. He is afraid for them, knowing the way men think, for the dangers aren't always imaginary. But the breaking point arrives when he finds out that his daughter has been flirting with a non-Muslim. He nearly collapses from a heart attack, doesn't know how to react. Back home he would have locked her up and beat her, as in the past, or killed her outright. The idea has crossed his mind of imposing an arranged marriage on her with another Muslim, but he would be acting contrary to the law and even against the wishes of his own family, not to mention the exhausting struggle with his young daughter. Even harder to explain is the fact that the girls are wilder than the boys, freer with respect to religion and tradition: they have nothing to lose but their chains.

This lack of understanding between the generations can become antagonistic, openly hostile, contemptuous. The

THE IMMIGRANT

son does not fear the police like his father, who retains the reflexes of an immigrant. Instead he provokes them, throws stones at them, knowing that in a democratic country he is not risking much. More often he will become a delinquent, a small-time supplier of soft drugs like hashish, and sometimes even hard drugs—cocaine and heroin for the most part. Sometimes he will practice a particularly odious form of extortion on his classmates. He's not alone, delinquency is not an exotic specialty, but it flourishes among the disaffected. And since the percentage of unemployed and poor is greater among the children of immigrants, delinquency is greater as well. This correlation becomes an overriding factor in the minds of many.

The immigrant father is ashamed, even though he pretends to protect the delinquents in his community. He disapproves of the young man smoking in the subway, knowing it is illegal, who verbally mocks the disapproval shown on the faces of the other passengers. He is scandalized by the differences in language, even though he tries to attenuate them; his wife especially, who defends the children. He is furious and frightened because he feels that everything he has so laboriously constructed is being called into question. For his efforts he experiences resentment and the barely concealed contempt of his children, who like all children would have preferred a father with somewhat greater prestige. But now the difference between them and this "old man" who repeats the stories of his hometown and has "cleaned other people's shit" for so many years is simply too great. How could he have accepted it? They forget that there were few jobs available then and that if he hadn't done what he did, they wouldn't be here.

The son is a rebel, in both his father's eyes and his own. He doesn't yet know what to do with his rebelliousness, but he refuses to identify with his father, whose salary has become

THE IMMIGRANT

laughable compared to the family's needs. Besides, there are other sources of income, most importantly the sale of hashish, which is far more remunerative than the others. If he has the misfortune to lose his job, he will become just another mouth to feed. The mother sometimes benefits from the shortcomings of the father; the son rarely speaks about the man, who is scorned and still feared, as if he were absent, by his mother. But because she is overweight, illiterate, and dresses differently, she deviates too much from the model of the Western woman—thin and elegant—he hopes to conquer (without always acknowledging it) and whom the daughters openly imitate.

The immigrant's son is a new man in Europe, still in the process of being born, who doesn't know himself who he is, who doesn't know exactly what he wants to become. It is never easy to feel ashamed of one's parents and, at the same time, to have doubts about one's future. The Italian, Jewish, Russian, and Polish immigrants who reached France felt a mixture of gratitude and irritation for the country because they were slow to obtain what they sought, but they were aware of what they wanted and struggled to achieve it. While all exiles live out a troubled identity, not all of them are children of a father who has been colonized by the country that has become, for better or worse, their own. The son of the Maghrebi immigrant must digest the memory of colonial domination and the exploitation that followed from within the former colonial power.

The Zombie

Who is he, then? What do we call him? The absence of a clear definition indicates his difficulty at integrating with anything: with his family, where the depressive and humiliated father,

115

THE IMMIGRANT

with his periodic lapses into an aggressive silence, has discovered alcohol, and through it a restored sense of disruptive vigor and a semblance of authority; and with a community, itself subject to identity problems. He even refers to himself as a *beur*, a slang anagram of the French "*arabe*," but this means defining himself as a foreigner to the nation, French and Christian, clinging to his ethnic and Muslim origins. *Jeunes Maghrébins* was hardly any better since it was still, in a sense, a form of exclusion, an insistence on difference. That is why the children of immigrants have been reduced simply to being young, or *jeunes*, in reference solely to their age, even though theirs was a very special kind of youth, which did not share the criteria, the concerns, and the future of other young people. This served to excuse their rowdy demonstrations, their spontaneous solidarity with the mistakes of their friends, their permanent revolt against the police, the violence of their reactions to the slightest restriction. And since they were not fated to remain young, a more general term was needed, so someone suggested *French Muslims,* without realizing just what those two words implied.

Because of their color young blacks in France experience additional complexity; they are unstable, agitated, dissatisfied with themselves and the entire world. They are often in conflict with the *beurs*, although they share a number of their frustrations and demands; they reject the image of themselves they see in one another. Then there is the old and still unresolved traditional Arab disdain for former slaves, and the vague rancor of the blacks toward slave traders. *Beur* on black violence, moreover, is commonplace. Only the Antillais, assured of their longevity in the French-speaking community, have escaped this malaise, this doubt about oneself and others, even though they also refer to the color of their skin and, in the recent past, have been susceptible to calls for inde-

116

THE IMMIGRANT

pendence. The *blacks*, as they refer to themselves, like their comrade *beurs*, show just as little indulgence toward their parents or their community. They despise the docile, self-effacing Senegalese or Malian workers, little inclined to rebelliousness, who supply the ranks of the infantry (even though, contrary to popular belief, they have often rebelled against the draft) and are the first sent into battle. Upon their return they are rewarded with a medal and a job as a street sweeper or sewer cleaner.

The *beur*, like the black, refuses to be a street sweeper or sewer cleaner. So what will he be? To avoid being relegated to the bottom of the social ladder, in a country where a diploma has replaced the birth privilege of the ancien régime, you must have an education. Yet, his revolt extends to the educational institutions that characterize the society he lives in. He will arrive late and create disturbances, seeing school as a symbol of control, placing the unfortunate teachers, full of good intentions, in an untenable situation. Order in school is based on respect for teachers. How can you teach a class where there is no authority to speak of? Where snickering has taken the place of consent, where obscenity, insult, and sometimes violence have replaced the traditional relationship between student and teacher; where the students do as they please, refusing to learn certain subjects? But the rejection of education, which might have saved the immigrant's son, becomes an aspect of his self-destruction. The young man who thought he could challenge the system, who has reduced his father to the role of a street sweeper, risks being reduced in turn and joining the hated paternal figure. Add to this the xenophobia prevalent in hiring and it's easy to see why 40 percent of those under twenty-five living in the ghettos are unemployed and susceptible to the kinds of transgressive behavior and mischief that typify the unemployed young. Wandering around in groups or gossiping in public squares or the hallways of buildings, they arouse the apprehension of nonimmigrants, whom they periodically ridicule.

A handful of generous institutions, unions and left-wing political parties, could have served as the outlet for this impatience. If they had made efforts to assist the disenfranchised, they would have had access to a new client base. For a time, socialism appeared to be the best option for immigrants and their children, as it did for the third world as a whole. This was an opportunity for another misunderstanding. The socialists, in the broad sense of the term, failed to appreciate the specific conditions of immigrant life, as well as those of the third world in general. They scarcely considered the ethnic, national, and religious dimensions. They had an excuse of sorts in that they were themselves critics of such factors. Primarily concerned with the interests of their own constituency, they sometimes shared their prejudices. A Communist mayor used a bulldozer to knock down a building that had been built, illegally, by immigrants. Right or wrong, the immigrant came away with the impression that those institutions failed to show the same determination in their struggle against employment discrimination. To the detriment of third-world nations, Communists and their union allies often focused on the protection of the USSR, the "homeland of socialism," which was more willing to supply them with arms—sold at top dollar—than food and technical assistance. Consequently, the son of the immigrant concluded that, in the current environment, institutions took care of everything except him and his problems.

There were meetings with other "brothers," where the immigrant was finally able to speak of his deepest concerns. But aside from shared anger over the Palestinian problem and hatred of America, or the desire to live in some imaginary

THE IMMIGRANT

country, a mythical Africa for the blacks, Andalusia for the Arabs, they were faced with a series of dead ends, which simply confirmed their exclusion from day-to-day society. Those sterile and endless palavers produced no rational solution. Fed up, the young man returned to his state of idleness.

The son of the immigrant is a kind of zombie, lacking any profound attachment to the land in which he was born. He is a French citizen but does not feel in the least bit French; he shares only partially the culture of the majority of the population and certainly not their religion. For all that, he is not completely Arab. He barely speaks the language, which is still used by his parents, to whom he answers in French or some blend of the two incomprehensible to outsiders. At school he rarely chooses Arabic as a second language. If he turns to religion, he would be hard pressed to read the Koran he waves around during demonstrations like a flag, similar to the head scarf worn by young women. If he travels to his parents' homeland, he discovers the extent to which it is not his own. And he would never dream of moving there, as if he were the inhabitant of another planet.

And, in truth, he is from another planet: the ghetto. Those who extol the romanticism of the ghetto have no idea what they're talking about. They must be confusing Sceaux, discreet and elegant, covered with greenery, with Choisy-le-Roi, in ruins, abandoned by the gods and the politicians, yet only a few kilometers from the capital. Living in a poor suburb is like living in another city, with its dilapidated buildings, dangerous elevators, plywood doors covered with peeling paint, broken sidewalks covered with mud in winter and sunbaked in summer. The suburban ghetto is a desert without a center, where there are few cafés and the stores are dirty. Anyone who is in the least bit successful moves out, so that the concentration of poverty and problems remains unchanged. It is a place where the police are reluctant to enter because of the anger they arouse among the "youth," as if this territory were a no-man's-land that belonged to them and would be violated by the enemy; a place where the forces of order, frustrated by the incessant difficulty of their task and the constant questioning of their authority, do not always show the tact they manifest in upscale neighborhoods. When these "kids" come into the city, the city of the well-off, to escape their world, it is as if they had gone on an expedition—they are amazed, envious, aggressive. And when they return, they are filled with the melancholy of those who return from a vacation cut short.

From Exclusion to Delinquency

Having refused to identify with his parents, believing he has been rejected by the majority, the only alternative for the son of an immigrant is to exist on his own. He must seek a model elsewhere than in the social majority, outside the borders. But this other identification presents difficulties of its own. Naturally, he's not going to mimic foreign conservatives, from whom he would experience the same rejection. Rather, he seeks support among the opposition and the marginalized, in what is referred to as the subculture, preferably American, and principally among blacks. This gives rise to another paradox since he is borrowing an identity of sorts from a hated America, although from its challengers. Such is the attraction of the dominant civilization that it fascinates even those it dominates.

Thus a portrait begins to appear of the son of the immigrant, a snapshot of sorts, easily recognizable. T-shirt in summer, leather jacket in winter, bought at a discount, often a pair of baggy pants that fall to his knees, interfere with his walking

THE IMMIGRANT

and leave him looking like a sheep when viewed from behind. The look is similar to the Arab *sarwal*, which can still be seen as far as Muslim Chad. Drawing on American black culture, he does not realize that those same blacks have drawn inspiration from Africa, not only because of the color of their skin but because, feeling they remain dominated by whites after having been slaves, they believe that is where their pre-slave origins can be found. For the same confused reason, some cut their hair in a kind of cockscomb, imitating the South American tribes decimated by the Spanish invaders. In May 1968 some of the demonstrators, criticized by the students for their gratuitous violence, wearing fur hats and chains, referred to themselves as "Afghans" because they represented—or so they thought—absolute revolt. The multitude of fine braids known as "cornrows" is also of African origin via America. Piercing and tattooing are endemic to the entire youth population. Arab-Muslims, as well as European sympathizers of the Palestinian struggle, wear a black-and-white (or black-and-red, as is common in the Middle East) scarf around their neck. On their head they wear a baseball cap, preferably backwards, a look that is now being adopted by a number of people because of its convenience and the American influence. These are not only fashions, as with the young of the majority population, who are subject to a certain third-world influence (for example, in their music), but signs of ostentation, which extend to their rolling gait, a bit like a sailor or boxer, probably to give the impression of greater physical presence, self-control, and strength.

For the same likely reason, the immigrant's son will travel in a group, as adolescents often do, to escape his loneliness and gain strength from the presence of his friends. Here he is no longer an individual but the member of a formidable clan, one that instills real fear. But the fear they inspire is a

THE IMMIGRANT

source of pleasure, a provocation, and a suggestion of control over those outside the clan. For the immigrant's son it is also a form of revenge. To compensate for the many times his father beat him with a broomstick on the sidewalk, which he now fills with his companions, he forces other pedestrians to walk in the street. He will make as much noise as possible, talk loudly, in Arabic if he can. He refuses to step aside for anyone, even an elderly woman, who must flatten herself against the wall, because the elderly are also the enemy.

He nonchalantly walks against red lights to force drivers to slow down. In the subway he jumps the turnstile, with the added pleasure of displaying his agility. He puts his feet on the seat opposite, tags the window with his signature. Judging that the laws were not made for him but against him, he feels he doesn't have to respect them.

In contrast, he will have his own rituals, which are, for the most part, displays of protest and provocation, if not outright aggression. Even dancing and music assume this significance. Hip-hop, rap, and tagging, all imported from America, are symbolic of this. In hip-hop, half dance, half acrobatics, the dancers, using their hands, revolve, like a top, around their head, which serves as a pivot. Rap, a syncopated form of speech, sometimes accompanied by music and a likely reflection of African griots, is the verbal substitute for violence against what he considers to be the institutional violence of the majority. Tagging goes one step further. A mixture of graffiti and drawing that is often playfully inventive, it appears on walls, cars, trains, even out-of-the-way locations, intruding into the world of the majority, which is forced to look at these unwanted messages. Likewise, though devoid of the aesthetic element, scribbling on street signs, urinating in elevators, and slashing subway and bus seats serve the same function. Take this one step further

THE IMMIGRANT

and you start setting fire to automobiles—more than twenty a night are burned in France, and more than three hundred on New Year's Eve.

There have been no terrorist attacks yet, but there is an obvious gradation in the level of delinquency. Insults such as "fuck your mother!" or "fuck your sister" seek to touch the majority where it is most sensitive, female sexuality, especially when expressed by someone from a culture that assigns so much importance to the virtue of its own women. On a collective level, there was an incident where, at a large French stadium, the children of immigrants whistled when the "Marseillaise," the French national anthem, was sung, indicating their hostility to an entire nation. In response they cried out, "We are all bin Laden," "We are all Saddam," thereby affirming what they believe to be their true allegiance—to a foreigner in conflict with the West. Or consider this threat: "There are six million of us; in twenty years there will be ten million!" We'll just have to wait and see....

But while delinquency is an attempt to affect the established order, it becomes self-destructive, for society will eventually defend itself. An altercation with the police involving a stolen car can turn into a catastrophic encounter, which triggers a cycle of reprisals and counterattacks. These serve to confirm the feeling of exclusion and bring about new provocations and worse delinquency. The prisons are full of petty criminals, small-time dealers, shoplifters, brawlers, strutting macho types who rape young women from the ghetto. Yet they are only a minority. It is likely that Western governments prefer not to clamp down on the kind of petty trafficking that feeds thousands of people; moreover, effective repression would lead to other forms of delinquency. There are few individuals who are seriously violent, whether criminal or political, but what do you do with the ones who punch old

THE IMMIGRANT

women in the face and steal their purse? Is it surprising that it is among such immigrant children that suicide bombers are recruited? That resentment nourishes terrorism?

Questioning Integration

And yet, in spite of everything, the most reasonable approach when living in a foreign environment would be the fullest integration possible with the majority population, at least in appearance. For centuries the Marranos in Spain pretended to practice Catholicism to escape the wrath of the Inquisition. But neither men nor history are simply reasonable. For assimilation to succeed, it requires that the minority desires it and that the majority agrees. Yet in the case of the immigrant, like that of the native, this is far from obvious; both fear it as much as they seem willing to accept it.

For the immigrant, the native's attitude is ambiguous. When he was a colonizer he was good at guessing the feelings of the colonized; on occasion he even sympathized with their problems. If, following some reversal, he was occasionally in danger, it was a danger he understood. If he himself had been dominated, perhaps he would have reacted the same way. It was simply his good fortune to be part of a powerful nation, to be protected by a police force and an army outfitted for effective repression. Yet paradoxically, he no longer understands his former adversary, now his fellow citizen. Before, it was clear. The immigrant demanded his independence and he got it. So what does he want now? Moreover, why didn't he stay where he was, to enjoy a freedom that was bought at such a great price? Why did he hurry to reach the former colonizer's land he claimed to hate, from which he wanted to separate at any price? Furthermore, why, since he claims to be miserable there, doesn't he go back to his liberated country?

124

THE IMMIGRANT

Obviously, it's not as simple as that. Years of cohabitation between colonizer and colonized have created bonds—economic, linguistic, cultural, even familial sometimes. Then there are the economic and political difficulties experienced by the young nation, many of which, the immigrant claims, are the result of occupation. The majority may concede this, but then why not assimilate completely, sincerely, rather than remain a stranger of sorts? During the colonial era, with everyone living among their own people, there was little mutual understanding; now a shared life requires that they get to know one another. Those in the majority have the impression of confronting a being with two faces, one familiar, the other unknown, which it must, for better or worse, confront. To eliminate the sense of foreignness that has slipped into their life, they perceive no other solution than the radical transformation of the minority population, so that it will ultimately resemble their own.

Yet this may not be possible. It's not even certain that they want it. Like any foreigner, the immigrant is perceived as a potential traitor. At best he experiences a kind of double loyalty: toward his country of origin and toward the host country. Should a crisis arise between these two, it's unclear how he would react, which he would betray. When in doubt, it's better to keep an eye on things. During the Second World War, the United States, just in case, placed U.S. citizens of Japanese origin in internment camps, people who had done nothing to arouse suspicion. The French did the same with the Italians, even the antifascists. Young nations, including Israel, prefer to excuse their minorities from military service—in other words, access to weapons. During the Iraq war, Europe breathed a sigh of relief given the relative calm among its Muslim communities. But didn't this presume that the potential to cause unrest was a reality? That their solidarity with a Muslim country might have gotten the better of them? The immigrant community is suspected of jeopardizing the cohesion, if not the interests, of the host country. It is like a Trojan horse, its belly filled with armed combatants who, on a signal from without, spread through the city to open the gates to the assailant.

This is something new in the history of Europe. It is not the first time it has played host to foreigners, but to assimilate them, it must not only welcome them but have the capacity to absorb them. This time it is doubtful that it can, or even that it wants to. The "yellow peril" has given rise to the "Muslim peril," in the face of which the majority population feels helpless. The French, and European, majority is not certain it is capable of absorbing the Muslim immigrant, the way it absorbed—without too much difficulty—Polish miners and Italian and Portuguese masons. Moreover, it would require that France continue to believe in the density, the primacy of its culture and values, something that has become increasingly doubtful. Although few may remember, it wasn't so long ago that French schools promoted the idea of a common ancestry from the Gauls. This annoyed some and amused others, but eventually everyone more or less accepted it—except for the recent immigrant and his children. No one would dare make such a claim today. On the contrary, the government fears that in instituting language and civilization courses the schools are operating counter to the rights and desires, the collective personality of immigrants. This has resulted in the educational weakness of the former colonial power. Once again the blame fell on the unfortunate educators, who were unable to change the situation. As if, without saying so openly, no one believed that the new immigrants could be assimilated.

It's true that to be assimilated you must first be assimilable.

THE IMMIGRANT

But, in the face of the fears, real or imaginary, of the assimilator, there exist the corresponding fears of the candidate for assimilation—the refusal of the one is matched by the resistance of the other. Faced with the needs of the majority, the minority panics, as if it were standing on the edge of a precipice. The polemic on assimilation and integration is not simply semantic: How far can and should the immigrant go to convince others of his good intentions? Is it enough that he is integrated superficially, and can he do so while retaining a sufficient sense of identity?

The Italians, Portuguese, Spanish, and soon the Romanians and Hungarians, all European and Christian, became part of a parish, a step on the path to assimilation. Martínez became Martinet, then Martin. The Muslim immigrants remain Muslims and continue to call themselves Mohammed and Ali, thus are visibly and deliberately different and separate. Islam is not only a religion, it is a culture and a civilization that encompass the social and even the political. This was the case with Christianity, but the majority of Europeans, including believers, have won the right of not having to subject the entirety of their life to their church. Islam, a relatively young religion, and therefore more demanding, even in its ideology, has not yet accomplished this separation. It remains both prophecy and legislation; the civil code and the religious code coincide. What is to be done when the laws of the Republic clash with those of religion? How can we balance concessions to the majority with unconditional submission to a tradition? Any deviation appears as a betrayal, which creates a feeling of guilt: distancing himself from religion, the assimilated individual believes he has abandoned his people.

Mixed marriages, the most common method of joining the majority, now become a question of loss or competition.

THE IMMIGRANT

The immigrant wouldn't dream of calling his son Pierre or Paul, which for many recall Saint Peter and Saint Paul. At most, his children might be given ambiguous names: Gaïs or Kalis for boys, Nadia or Sophia for girls. The ideal situation would be for the spouse to renounce his or her own religion and convert to Islam, which many families demand and obtain before giving their consent. In this way they gain a Muslim instead of losing one. But once again they are turning their back on immigration.

Reciprocal Dependence

So, what should we do? By "we" I mean all the inhabitants of the planet, for this question affects all of us, former oppressors, formerly oppressed, and even those who believe they remain outside history. For that matter, to have succeeded in attracting the world's attention would be one of the most solid accomplishments of the decolonized. Until now relations among the various peoples have taken the form of permanent battles between rival bands, dressed in different uniforms, each of them invoking their god to obtain his assistance and justify his pillage. Morality, religion, and law were attempts to attenuate widespread savagery by ritualizing it. The Ten Commandments, God's judgment, human rights, the status of prisoners of war—all were stages in this effort. Simultaneously, even as late as the eighteenth century, travelers were abducted on the high seas and kept as hostages for ransom. The French or English corsair was no less cruel than the Barbary pirate ship. Such activities continue in Africa and Asia, where slavery has not disappeared. Europe has only recently surrendered its colonies, which were often forms of collective slavery. There was little hesitation in burning or razing towns that resisted the will of the invader. We behaved similarly dur-

128

THE IMMIGRANT

ing the last war. Modern wars, although they appear in more noble guise, are simply plunder on a larger scale.

We have just made an important discovery: we now live within a state of previously unknown dependence. Until now we had little need of one another, except for purposes of mutual victimization. Navigation and caravans ensured the exchange of rare products, spices, and precious metals. Now the speed of communication and global competition have resulted in general interdependence. Clearly, we need to control globalization, ensure that it does not sideline the most fragile, but no one can turn the clock backward. Antiglobalization is a trap. The West has discovered that it cannot live peacefully if the majority of the world's inhabitants live in poverty, envious of the developed world. Because of its very progress, the West has become a fat glutton; it stuffs itself with food and destroys its toys like a spoiled child. With the exception of a small number of absurd and scandalous pockets of poverty—among the elderly, for example—it resembles a giant Club Med that discards excess food while the surrounding villages go hungry.

Even scattered violence encourages such solidarity. The tragedy of September 11, 2001, acted a bit like an electrical shock: the ruling powers discovered they were no longer certain of their ability to ensure their own security. The time is over when they could, with their peers, share the empire of the world and rule according to their own interests. Already the upheavals of decolonization have revealed their limitations. No matter how much they might wish to reexperience their former self-sufficiency, they cannot, given the scope of their economic and political involvement with the rest of the world. But from this point of view, those once dominated must recognize that they too can no longer live outside the world; otherwise they risk returning to the Middle Ages, forced to reject the technical, scientific, and medical progress of the West. Now everyone must work to organize this irreversible interdependence for our mutual benefit, at least if we wish to live in a less stressful and less dangerous world.

The Languors of Europe

There has been renewed talk of a decline of the West, including the United States of America, an idea that has been around for decades. The West doesn't seem to be doing all that badly when you consider that the distance between it and the rest of the world remains considerable. Populations are moving westward rather than eastward. Third-world students prefer to study in Western universities. Prosperity is increasing in the West, which is rarely the case elsewhere. It's true, of course, that a civilization's high and low points are often contiguous: Rome was at the height of its power when it began its decline; Constantinople, which took over from Rome, was razed by the Turks. Closer in time, prior to its fall, the Austro-Hungarian Empire seemed to be invulnerable; the USSR, the second leading world power, has collapsed. Who will be next? Such is the wheel of history, which raises a nation up only to cast it into the shadows, leaving room for another to come along. It could be said that Europe is a depressed sovereign in a state of torpor and that this is not a sign of good health. The sickness comes from afar. Notwithstanding its brilliant successes, Europe has continued to self-destruct. The Napoleonic era left France drained. The First World War deprived France and Germany of the creative energies of a generation; the Second World War was worse, since it weakened the entire continent. It should come as no surprise that it suffers from a case of pernicious anemia. This has clearly manifested itself during the subsequent colonial conflicts; and it required

THE IMMIGRANT

the help of the Americans, in the form of the Marshall Plan, to restart the European economy after World War II. The diseases now eating away at it are recognizable and can be summarized as follows: demographic exhaustion, immigration, mixed marriage.

The demographic problem has continued unabated and has possibly worsened. This may be the sign of a natural decline of European society, like those packs of whales that show up one day, without any apparent reason, to collapse and die onshore. Or, less mysteriously, women's participation in the labor force and social activities, which is certainly legitimate, has allowed them less time for childbearing. Since women cannot physically work and raise children at the same time, and since society has provided no means for helping them manage such contradictory needs, they have chosen not to give birth. The result, with the help of progress in medicine, is the general aging of the population. This has resulted in an inability to ensure the self-regulation necessary for simple survival such as pension plans, health care, or the fulfillment of the simplest tasks, which our spoiled youth no longer want any part of. How can a society overcome this dilemma except by relying on immigration? Following the lead of industry and its need for labor, and wary of upsetting the voters, politicians have adopted a policy of ambiguity. The problem of immigration is, however, simple. The old, rich countries need to import a demographic component, and the poor countries need to export some of their unemployed—and potentially disorderly—youth. What can be done to address this situation?

Immigration also results in mixed marriages, and we may have entered an era of widespread intermarriage. It's possible that intermarriage is already implicitly accepted by the West, without its being aware of the social, political, and cultural consequences on the actual physiognomy of Western nations.

THE IMMIGRANT

The recent polemic in Italy, the Vatican stronghold, about the complaint of a Muslim convert who protested the presence of the crucifix in schools is typical. Perhaps intermarriage would have been more easily accepted by Europe, as it has been until now, if it was still equipped with a system of values in which it strongly believed and which guided its behavior. But the two major ideologies that have concerned Western intellectuals and influenced their behavior, Christianity and Marxism, are moribund. For a likely majority of the population, Christianity is no more than a ritual, at best a cultural background, hardly more influential than Hellenism. Jupiter, Venus, and Hercules are nearly as familiar, nearly as present in language as the Christian saints. The popes continue to call for the evangelization of the world, as if China, India, or Black Africa, where Islam stopped the expansion of Christianity, didn't exist. But who is listening? Marxism is no longer under consideration, at least in its Communist forms. It had promised economic prosperity and intellectual freedom for all men and instead brought famine, totalitarianism, and the camps. One wonders if the Marxists, like the Christians, still believe in a real future. This has led to the collapse of Communist parties and the utopian resurrection of the Trotskyists with their archaic, if not retrograde, avant-garde. After being consistently mistaken about Stalin, Tito, Castro, Mao, even Khomeini, they are now turning the revolutionary mission the former proletariat wants no part of over to the people of the third world. It's hard to be a revolutionary when you're well fed and healthy, when you own your own apartment, a car, and sometimes even a house in the country. But for the moment, the third world has chosen nationalism rather than socialism, religion rather than Enlightenment philosophy.

This is the void that Muslim fundamentalists have come to believe they can fill. Europe no longer defends itself spiri-

132

THE IMMIGRANT

tually or even militarily since it has turned over its defense to the United States and because there is no one capable of embracing the complexities of the new situation, much less of proposing a solution. In the face of an Islam that is sure of its values because of its relative youth, Europe no longer has a system of ethics capable of providing new guidelines. Skeptical and blasé like the elderly, it promotes an easygoing leniency, but the lack of civic pride is not freedom but anarchy. In every field of endeavor Europe has allowed itself simply to circumvent obstacles, while waiting for the oil wells to dry up and new forms of energy to be discovered. But it is far from clear that such procrastination will suffice to calm the impatience of the third world and the deadly passion of extremists.

In short, like a ping-pong match, the decolonized's chances lie principally with the weakness of the ex-colonizer. Assuming, however, that he doesn't play as badly as his adversary and partner.

Hope for the Decolonized?

I'd like to review the pluses and minuses of the situation. In general, the third world is still afflicted with crushing poverty, corruption, and despotism, which produce cultural sterility, humiliation, resentment, and, eventually, violence. This assessment is now recognized even by the handful of third-world intellectuals who dare to speak out—their societies are sick.

However, there is no shortage of benefits. These countries possess immense wealth distributed over vast land areas, large populations that enable them to compensate for the West's declining birthrates, and a diplomatic and military presence that has become a force to be reckoned with on the interna-

THE IMMIGRANT

tional scene. Even though, with the complicity of the rich, that wealth has often been transformed into a brake on the development of the countries that control it. Their ever-expanding population, which allows them to exert pressure on the West, has also become a growing embarrassment for underdeveloped countries. International organizations, which might have been able to establish genuine international law by developing instruments suited to its application and enforcing sanctions against those who fail to abide by it—without which the law remains ineffective—have rapidly been transformed into combat zones in which conflicts of interest, dubious coalitions, and relations of force are played out.

Nonetheless, we cannot reproach the third world for not having sought out the development models that might have allowed it to escape such dead ends. There have been two primary models, with a number of variants: economic liberalism and Marxist socialism. Yet until now both have been sources of disappointment.

Economic liberalism projects a multiplication of consumer goods and their widespread distribution through free trade, all of which are supported by political democracy. What is there to criticize in such a program, assuming it could be fully realized? Unfortunately, it assumes that there is relative equality between partners, which is very far from being the case, both within nations and among them. In spite of substantial progress, poverty continues to affect the majority of third-world countries. Those who have chosen economic liberalism have not experienced any appreciable development, quite the contrary. In the jungle that governs international economic relations, a fragile third world is constantly shattered against the iron first of capitalist commerce. The third world is not equipped for such freedom, which always benefits the most powerful.

THE IMMIGRANT

Those who have experimented with Communism, or communizing experiences, have fared no better. Vietnam, which for a while seemed to be the most successful representative of the Communist world, resigned itself to living from hand to mouth. North Korea is impoverished while capitalist South Korea is prosperous. With the exception of South Africa, where the Marxist African National Congress (ANC) participates in the government, no African or Asian Communist Party has been able, without the protection of the Soviet Union, to retain power for any length of time. Should we be surprised that the competition between Communism and traditional structures, promoted by the resistance of feudal leaders, has regularly ended in the victory of tradition?

Nor can we reproach the leaders of the third world for having sought alternative solutions to the above, which seemed to be specifically Western. In spite of appearances, Europe intends to remain Christian. Marxism has been transformed into a new religion, dogmatic and exclusive, but without the habitual appeal of religion: the reassuring rituals and mythic hopes. But if it's a question of religion, why not simply return to one's own, to which one is, after all, viscerally attached? In Latin America, Christian renewal movements like "liberation theology" represent a return to the letter of the Gospels, as if, by means of the sacred texts, God was guiding the revolutionaries. In the Arab-Muslim world fundamentalism is a theological and political attempt to resolve every problem by a return to a pure, primitive tradition. But the very idea of a return illustrates the weakness of such attempts; we can never return anywhere.

Fundamentalism is pointlessly regressive, totalitarian, and repressive. Liberals and Marxists possess a universalist ambition, one that is even divorced from their interests; fundamentalism turns its back on such acquisitions: a generalized

135

THE IMMIGRANT

system of education that at least aspires to be neutral, the promotion of the individual, freedom of thought, the importance of the economy, the introduction of women into social life. The standard formula of the Egyptian "Muslim Brotherhood," the Iranian followers of Khomeini, and Palestine's Hamas—"Everything is in the Koran"—summarizes the ambitions and limitations of fundamentalism. Quite obviously, everything can't be contained in a text written several centuries ago, even when accompanied by its commentaries. The same is true for the Gospels or the Torah. Aside from a handful of general principles, we are advised to trust in the "law of God," that is, the injunctions of priests, who are not primarily experts in contemporary problems. Since God is always and inevitably right, why bother with human laws, which are fragile and changing? But by the same token, fundamentalism turns away from the search for adequate solutions to the current situation. "I am a Muslim before being a nationalist," said Ben Bella, the first president of the Algerian republic. In doing so he trivialized the nation's specific problems, primarily the economy, which turned out to be disastrous. The return to the traditional values of Islam appears to be more important than economic development. Despite whatever charitable goodwill it shows, fundamentalism ends up preserving the privileges of feudal lords and the wealthy.

Far from being a model that would beneficially replace the two others, fundamentalism is even more inadequate as a solution given the scope of the problems now facing Islam and the world. The return to Islam is, on the contrary, a form of totalitarian isolation. Like all fanaticism, it uses its totality as a bulwark against the outside world, considered to be a hostile and polluting totality, from which one's own people must be protected, even if it means fighting those who remain irresolute. Unable to satisfy desires, it is austere and demands

THE IMMIGRANT

austerity of everyone. However, since it cannot succeed by persuasion, it resorts to force. It attempts to control all aspects of individual and collective life, even so far as to pry into people's conscience. That is why it has such a hard time dealing with sexuality. It is even willing to consider the reconquest of the Earth to free it of heresy. To claim that everything resides in the Koran means there is nothing outside it; that anyone who does not follow the Koran falls outside the bounds of humanity and deserves to be treated with the utmost severity. Of course, such behavior is not limited to Islam. Christianity did the same until the separation of religion and politics, which resulted in the decisive democratization of Europe, critical freedom, and initiative, essential conditions for the development of science and technology. In short, fundamentalism is conducted, from within and without, as a form of continuous war.

Toward a New World

Can we, in spite of everything, hope for a different future, where we all manage to live in harmony? If so, what price would we have to pay to achieve this? For we are leaving the world of fact for the world of hopes and dreams. In *The Colonizer and the Colonized*, published by Beacon Press in 1991, I insisted on the necessity of such a distinction; here, I only wish to add that the following pages are based more on speculation than certainty.

I would again like to insist on one obvious fact, however: it is pointless to deplore the existence of poverty, it is now critical that we begin to counteract it. Those who do not take it seriously are not sincere participants in this global discussion. Naturally, poverty is not the only element at play here. We have already seen this in terms of decolonization, where

THE IMMIGRANT

national claims often took precedence over all others. Terrorists are often members of the upper class, both their leaders and their foot soldiers. But it is poverty that supplies the bulk of their supporters, and these are easy to deceive, uncontrollable, and ready for just about anything. How could those crowds of men and women, exasperated by their hunger for food and love, not be hysterical? Maybe one day we'll succeed in creating a society in which no one suffers from physical exhaustion. It is politically correct in the West to deplore the missteps of development and excess consumption. These, however, are the criticisms of the well-to-do, who denounce the excess from which they alone benefit. There is no need to have a television in every room or to buy a new car every year, but that is far from the situation throughout the world, where even the foods necessary for survival and basic medicines are lacking. Moreover, poverty is relative. When it coexists alongside wealth, it arouses envy and anger. While some sort of comprehensive regulation is needed, the condemnation of industrialization or scientific agriculture, which alone guarantee abundance, means abandoning people to their poverty and renouncing civilization.

However, we have yet to explain why the third world has failed to develop or has been so slow to do so. Of the two main tools for overcoming poverty—development and the struggle against corruption—it is unclear that the first alone is up to the task. During the failed meeting in Cancún, there was legitimate criticism by the various speakers of the harshness of international competition, especially between rich and poor nations, but none at all concerning the rampant corruption. That would have meant criticizing the leaders who represented them. And did we expect them to accuse themselves? Yet corruption is one of the major causes of third-world stagnation. It neutralizes any attempt

138

THE IMMIGRANT

at advancement and negates the results; its restraint on development is greater than the tendency of development to promote corruption. It is why wealth earned within a company is invested abroad, where it expands foreign financial markets or inflates the housing market in Western capitals. In this way entire streets in London, through the intermediary of dummy companies, have come under the ownership of third-world investors. There is objective complicity among the privileged, which extends beyond borders and continents. Why would they change a situation that benefits them? That would mean, as an example, revealing the complicated web of secrecy behind oil and politics. Money laundering does not only benefit the world's various mafias. What about bank profits? The United States, "promoter of democracy," Russia, once the "homeland of the worker," France, "the promoter of human rights," are, respectively, in exchange for substantial remuneration, the three leading global suppliers of arms, which are used to sow death and strengthen tyranny. All those resonant declarations of intent are nothing but hypocrisy if they do not succeed in reversing this unconscionable situation. What are we to think of those third-world leaders who spend enormous sums of money to buy arms instead of food and medicine, which they prefer to cajole from the developed nations? How can we dare speak of morality in international, even national, affairs given the way they are currently being managed?

We come now to the heart of the matter: nothing can replace a people's need for self-governance, as was shown during the various decolonization movements. They must recover their wealth and, to do that, begin by freeing themselves of the *raïs* and caudillos, the putschists and accomplices of the privileged, internal and external, of their *líder máximo*, the comic title given to Fidel Castro, and their "supreme combatants,"

139

THE IMMIGRANT

the paranoid title assumed by an aging Bourguiba, along with the political imams and compensatory myths that perpetuate stagnation and, sometimes, regression. Only a rediscovered freedom will create an environment where a pragmatic balance can be maintained between economic liberalism and a centralized economy based on actual circumstances and the specific needs of all individuals.

All else is illusory or unpredictable: "aid," "partnership," "debt elimination," and so on, even when not self-serving, which is doubtful. "Linked aid," for example, a concept of barely veiled cynicism, suggests that money is advanced providing you spend it on purchasing the lender's products, in other words, on the condition it is returned to the lender. The "partnerships" of which so much has been made lately have meaning only if the two partners are equally matched, which is precisely not the case; otherwise the views and interests of the stronger party will always prevail. "Debt elimination," though generous in appearance, merely delays the problem. What prevents the poor from borrowing again, and continuing their cycle of dependence on rich countries? The possibility of gain has made the lenders sloppy and the borrowers are deaf, since they know they will be unable to repay the loans. "Sharing," an idea that has been around for a long time, has been dusted off again. It is merely another word for charity, which has never solved anything. On the contrary, it simply perpetuates inequality. Waiting for salvation from a colonial power, now a former colonial power, is as illusory as it is for women to expect to attain their liberation through male goodwill. International aid is a form of disguised begging, but begging does not cure poverty; on the contrary, it simply promotes irresponsibility. Even more so since subventions manage to destroy the effects of international solidarity.

Humiliated, exasperated by problems with no viable

140

THE IMMIGRANT

solution, fundamentalists have opted for violent confrontation—war, a war they have no chance of winning. But although they cannot win the war, they can destroy peace. It's a foolish undertaking. For it would mean making the world unlivable for those they claim to defend. The hour has come for the Arab world to assume its proper place in the concert of nations. It has money, manpower, the support of other Muslim nations, positive global opinion. Why should it exhaust itself in a permanent conflict from which it has nothing more to gain? Fundamentalist activities are, outside their fantasies, in this sense catastrophic, and contrary to the very interests of the Arab peoples. Certainly the silent majority desires integration without excess upheaval; but it is often active minorities that make history if they are not restrained by the majority. Will the Arab-Muslim majority manage to make itself heard in the face of the activities of its fundamentalists? Will it persuade itself that their victory would plunge all of us into the shadows of history? Their intent is now obvious, and it is twofold: to destroy the Arab regimes one by one and, simultaneously, to harass the West until there is a global confrontation between it and the Arab-Muslim world. The fundamentalists have been relatively successful in creating a vicious circle: terror against the West generates suspicion of all Arabs and this suspicion feeds the resentment against the entire West. Will the Arab-Muslim majority manage to overcome this dilemma? In any event, it cannot live in symbiosis with the West and show indulgence toward those who desire its destruction. The normal and desirable destiny of any immigrant is to transform himself into a citizen, providing he does not appear to be an enemy in his host country.

If people were reasonable, even rational, they would see only their own interest, since they are destined to live together, to search out what unites them rather than what

141

THE IMMIGRANT

distinguishes them, or moves them apart, in other words, *common denominators*. This is not the place to exhaustively enumerate or provide a detailed exposition of what the practical modalities might be; we need to leave something for the politicians to do. Nor is it the intention of this book, which is primarily descriptive. However, I have suggested more than once that we must begin by eradicating extreme poverty through a more equitable distribution and better management of wealth—wealth that should belong to everyone and not to a select few, including natural energy. The radical suppression of corruption and despotism are the necessary conditions. The promotion of a universal morality obviously requires this. This morality will, of necessity, include secularism, for without it we will continue to have division and warfare. Secularism is not a ban on religious practice, which would be another form of tyranny. It is an institutional agreement to protect freedom of thought for everyone, including agnostics, against the interference of religious movements and the demands of fanatics. To accomplish this we must stop confusing religious membership and social membership, religion and culture, Islamic culture and Islamic demography. An Arab is not necessarily an Islamist believer, no more than a Jew is necessarily someone who regularly attends a synagogue, or a citizen a faithful churchgoer. We need to create a new terminology to express these distinctions. Secularism is the primary condition of true universalism, one that transcends singularities instead of tracking them. This implies the existence of a valid international system of law, one that is not manipulated as it so often is today, one to which local traditions and customs, although not ignored, are subject through the application of sanctions backed up by the forces to carry them out. Without these mechanisms, such law will be nothing more than an empty formality. To accomplish this

142

THE IMMIGRANT

program, we must convince ourselves of our solidarity. In the world that is being constructed day by day, no one can go it alone. Solidarity is not only a philosophical and moral concept, it is a practical necessity, without which our life would be one of continuous torment. And finally, to forestall the force of emotions and the blindness of prejudice, we must, to the extent possible, promote rationality, a condition for all the above, the mother of the advancement of the arts and sciences, even of a shared morality. The only workable solution would be the creation of a genuinely international body and the elimination of partisan organizations.

Would this really be the end of Western civilization? Perhaps, on the contrary, it would be the occasion for its true universalization. For the best aspects of the West will, of necessity, become part of a shared heritage. The third world must not reject these because they originated in the Western world. Should we reject algebra because it was transmitted to us by the Arabs? Printing because it was invented by the Chinese? These are shared discoveries and we should hope that they remain so. They include the promotion of the individual against the excessive control of groups, initiative, the product of liberty, progress, the product of both, the widespread humanization of relations between groups, equal opportunities for women, respect for minorities, universal education, progressive medical care, proportionality between crimes and their punishment—no one will continue to accept cutting off the hands of thieves or the lynching or stoning of women for adultery. And since this is primarily a portrait of the decolonized Arab-Muslim, Arab-Muslims must recognize and acknowledge—exactly contrary to fundamentalism—that the West is now a part of their world, just as the West must acknowledge that Muslims are now part of their world. Maybe one day there will be a Muslim mayor of Paris, as there have

THE IMMIGRANT

been Jewish mayors in New York. For that matter, why not a Jewish mayor in an Arab city?

But to achieve this utopia it is essential that the divide is no longer between Arab-Muslims as a whole and non-Muslims as a whole, but between both groups as a single coalition of free spirits against dogmatists and their fanaticism. For, all too often the partisans of God have "the devil in the flesh." Between these two categories of men, the same struggle needs to occur on a global scale, for our common salvation is at stake.

As I have mentioned earlier, such desires are utopian. Perhaps there is some naïveté in hoping that, in the near future, one group will succeed in tempering its resentment, the other its greed. Perhaps not enough time has elapsed from a world in which we could visit a Universal Exposition to see natives of foreign countries displayed like monkeys in a zoo, when we sang *Trabaja la mujer* and all the women were called Fatima and all the men Muhammad. It is still too soon for blacks to forget slavery and Jews the Shoah. It is not certain that the powerful of yesterday have truly understood that they must, from now on, do a better job of sharing wealth, even the wealth they themselves produce. Man is like every carnivore, he will jealously defend the hunk of meat between his paws. But to the first we must say again that one cannot live with resentment forever, especially if you wish to live elsewhere than your homeland; to the second that they will not be able to continue to tamp down the restlessness of the hungry and the humiliated. Maybe men are deaf and blind to certain evidence; maybe history, for the most part, simply passes us by and we have no other recourse than to let time pass, with the hope that things will improve. But if we can act toward fulfilling our shared destiny, even a little, if we can play some role in it, no matter how small, it would be unforgivable for us not to have tried.

144

Afterword

People, like events, are largely unpredictable. After writing this book, I was expecting a fairly emotional response from the community of the formerly colonized, especially Arab-Muslims. However, among my readers the ex-colonized and their descendants were apparently not scandalized, not even surprised by my project. On the contrary, it was as if they were expecting it. One of them, a television journalist, said to me, "There was a book to be written on this subject and you have written it." That is why, with the exception of a radio broadcast known for the violence of its sentiments, the media's reception has been generous and courteous. Radio Beur, BRTV, the Berber network, TV6, RFO all gave me considerable on-air time. The weekly *Jeune Afrique* devoted a full page to my book, *Afrique-Asie* a long article. Some of them were moved by my denunciation of the silence, not to mention the complicity, of most intellectuals, and pointed out to me the handful of courageous efforts by secular associations. I am encouraged by such efforts and hope that the number of such organizations continues to grow.

No, my greatest concern lies with the former colonizers themselves. I would be lying if I said that I didn't expect such a response from them; but although it served only to confirm

145

AFTERWORD

my suspicions, it nonetheless left behind a bitter aftertaste. I want to review here some of the more pathetic disavowals I encountered. A week after the appearance of the book, I received an invitation to speak on Radio Libertaire. The night before I was scheduled to go on, I received a phone call. The program had been canceled. Why? I was told, "Your comments are inappropriate for our listeners." "Maybe, but at least allow me to explain myself." The answer was no.

Libération sent a young man to interview me for an afternoon, but nothing came of it. I sent a note to the newspaper's editor. He didn't take the trouble to respond. He didn't have the courage to live up to his newspaper's promising name.

What did I say? What did I do? Did I make serious mistakes in reporting statistics, events, individuals? No. I had been careful, as I had in *The Colonizer and the Colonized*, to make use of the most reliable sources. I was forced to acknowledge that my readers were offended by my interpretation of the facts. I have written that the current misfortunes of third-world populations do not arise from the continued actions of their former colonizers, of neocolonialism, but principally from their new rulers, whose corruption and tyranny I have denounced. These rulers have kept their countries, even those rich in resources, in a state of paradoxical poverty, allowed customs to stagnate, and fostered mass emigration.

One would be forced to conclude that my criticism was unbearable. It was as if, by denouncing their rulers, I had insulted the people, which was exactly the opposite of my intent. For by illuminating these lapses, I believe, rather, that I have helped to demystify the situation. Therefore, I devoted exactly four pages to the conflict between Israel and Palestine. The subject is inexhaustible and convenient. I pointed out the deplorable situation of the Palestinians and urged the creation of a Palestinian state—something I have

AFTERWORD

done for thirty years, even when no one else was willing to do so, including the Arab states (see my *Juifs et Arabes* [Jews and Arabs], Gallimard, 1967). But I wondered why there had been such emphasis on the conflict, with its four thousand dead—deplorable like all deaths but hardly comparable to the millions of deaths in Africa, for example. As I write this afterword, a massacre in Darfur has left thirty thousand dead and displaced close to a million people. I have suggested that such chaos has been one of the most effective pretexts for tyrants to excuse their hold on power and the state of catalepsy in which they maintain their populations.

Not that the press has stinted on covering the book's publication, quite the contrary. It was well aware that I had formulated arguments that everyone was aware of but didn't want to discuss, and which my book exposed. So the press resorted to a stratagem. It acknowledged the event without revealing its content, with the exception of Jean Daniel, who, in his editorial, confirmed the accuracy of my descriptions. For the most part the press chose to speak about the author without discussing the book. Ultimately, the only person to really speak about the book was me, primarily through the many generous interviews I was offered. One of the most important was the interview with the perceptive and courageous Christian Makarian in *L'Express*, who allowed me to point out one of the major paradoxes in today's Western world. Namely, that at a time when the West's cultural, technological, even political values, its democracy, the condition of women, and the separation—at least relative—of church and state, are beginning to take root—legitimately—around the world, it finds itself violently challenged. Even *Le Monde*, which printed a full-page article about me by Catherine Simon, whom I cannot thank enough, emphasized the picturesque aspects of my life and work. But as for the book itself, the facts and their

AFTERWORD

interpretation, no more than a few lines appeared. There was nothing about the second generation, the children of immigrants, whom I discuss at length in the book. There was nothing about the two-sided resistance to integration we see in practice: the immigrants' hesitation to integrate and the host country's reluctance to integrate them. As if they preferred to leave me with the responsibility—which I assume, of course—and not mention facts that I would have preferred to see brought directly to the readers' attention.

I take some consolation in realizing that, aside from my disappointment as an author, this weighty silence suggests, on the contrary, the accuracy of my claims. This includes my remarks about the irresponsibility, if not blindness or cowardice, of many intellectuals, who have taken refuge in outdated theories instead of daring to confront a novel situation, and the inability of politicians to address, except rhetorically, the especially dangerous and irreversible turmoil in which the world now finds itself.

Paris, December 2004

ALBERT MEMMI was born and raised in Tunis, Tunisia, and lives in Paris. A novelist and critic, he has written extensively on colonialism, anti-Semitism, and racism. His books include *The Colonizer and the Colonized, Dominated Man, The Pillar of Salt,* and *Racism* (Minnesota, 2000). He is professor emeritus of sociology at the University of Paris, Nanterre.

ROBERT BONONNO has translated more than a dozen books, including Vincent Kaufmann's *Guy Debord: Revolution in the Service of Poetry* (Minnesota, 2006) and Henri Lefebvre's *The Urban Revolution* (Minnesota, 2003).